AMERICA the BEAUTIFUL
KANSAS

By Zachary Kent

Consultants

Betty Braddock, Director, Kansas Heritage Center, Dodge City

Robert L. Hillerich, Ph.D., Bowling Green State University, Bowling Green, Ohio

ℚ CHILDRENS PRESS®
CHICAGO

A Kansas farm in autumn

Project Editor: Joan Downing
Associate Editor: Shari Joffe
Design Director: Margrit Fiddle
Typesetting: Graphic Connections, Inc.
Engraving: Liberty Photoengraving

Library of Congress Cataloging-in-Publication Data

Kent, Zachary.
    America the beautiful. Kansas / by Zachary Kent.
        p.   cm.
    Includes index.
    Summary: Discusses the geography, history,
people, government, economy, and recreation of
Kansas.
    ISBN 0-516-00462-X
    1. Kansas—Juvenile literature. [1. Kansas]
I. Title.
F681.3.K46   1990   90-35385
978.1—dc20   CIP
                                       AC

Horses on a farm in the Flint Hills

TABLE OF CONTENTS

Chapter 1

MIDWAY, U.S.A.

MIDWAY, U.S.A.

"Take down your map, Sir," exclaimed Massachusetts Senator Charles Sumner in a famous 1856 congressional speech, "and you will find that the territory of Kansas . . . occupies the middle spot of North America . . . on the very highway between two oceans . . . calculated to nurture a powerful and generous people [and] worthy to be a central pivot of American Institutions."

Located at the very geographic heart of the continental United States, Kansas has proven Sumner's predictions totally correct. To people throughout the world, the image of wide-open Kansas fields of waving golden wheat is often the most enduring image of our country. The varied beauty and startling bounty of Kansas in both its countryside and cities can honestly be said to be the best reflection of all things American.

A land of social progress and agricultural and industrial productivity, Kansas owes its success to the spirit of its people. Survivors of a rich but hard pioneer heritage, Kansans meet their daily challenges with stubborn energy. Independent in thought and actions, Kansans remain different in backgrounds, interests, and goals. Yet they also often share traditional American virtues. Outspoken friendliness and warm hospitality greet visitors from north, south, east, and west as they cross into Kansas and enjoy the pleasures of "Midway, U.S.A."

Chapter 2
THE LAND

THE LAND

The soil itself is the most suitable that has been found for growing all the products of Spain, for, besides being rich and black, it is well watered by arroyos, springs, and rivers.
—Spanish explorer Francisco de Coronado following his 1541 journey through Kansas

The land that makes up Kansas boasts many striking features. Contrary to popular myth, the state is not simply one vast plain. Rivers twist and flow through a landscape of gently rolling hills and wide, shallow valleys. Farms and orchards offer vistas of lively color, and woods and flatlands still provide homes for wild plants and animals.

Kansas stretches 408 miles (657 kilometers) from east to west and 206 miles (332 kilometers) from north to south. On a map, the state looks like a rectangle with a bite taken out of its northeast corner, where the winding Missouri River forms part of the state's boundary with Missouri. Covering an area of 82,277 square miles (213,097 square kilometers), Kansas ranks fourteenth in size among the fifty states. A spot near Lebanon, in Smith County, marks the geographic center of the contiguous forty-eight states. Surveyors long ago marked a site farther southeast, in Osborne County, as the geodetic center of Canada, the United States, and Mexico. This means that it is the point of origin for all governmental mapping in North America.

Limestone ridges mark the rolling Flint Hills region.

TOPOGRAPHY

Kansas ranges in elevation from 680 feet (207 meters), in southeast Montgomery County; to 4,039-foot (1,231-meter) Mount Sunflower, in western Kansas's Wallace County. Through the centuries, ice, water, and wind have left their mark upon the surface of Kansas. Millions of years ago, much of southern and western Kansas lay beneath a great inland sea. Today, chalk beds along the Smoky Hill River reveal prehistoric fossils of strange fish, reptiles, and swimming birds. When the sea receded, it left behind the treeless High Plains section of western Kansas, which rolls gently downward into the Plains Border region in the central third of the state.

Great ice glaciers once scraped through the country of northeastern Kansas. They left behind rich topsoils and rocky river bluffs in this Dissected Till Plains region. The Flint Hills, an area of limestone ridges, signal a traveler's arrival into east-central

A Kansas farmstead

Kansas. The bluestem grass that grows abundantly here provides ranchers with fine grazing lands. The plains east of the Flint Hills make up the Osage Plains region.

RIVERS AND LAKES

All of the rivers in Kansas flow eastward until they finally drain into the mighty Mississippi River. The Missouri, Kansas, and Arkansas rivers are the state's most important waterways. Other well-known rivers include the Verdigris, Neosho, Marais des Cygnes, Republican, Solomon, Smoky Hill, and Cimarron. The Saline River earned its unusual name because of the high salt content of its waters. Another strange river is the White Woman Creek, which disappears in Scott County and flows underground

Ottawa State Fishing Lake near Minneapolis

for a distance. In all, there are some fifteen hundred named streams in Kansas. Most are shallow and choked by sandbars. Only the Missouri River is considered deep enough to support much commercial river traffic.

Almost all of the large lakes in Kansas are the result of river-damming projects. Twenty-five federal reservoirs, built to provide flood control, irrigation, and city water supplies, can be found in Kansas. Milford Lake on the Republican River, covering 16,000 acres (6,475 hectares), is the largest. Other man-made lakes include Perry Lake, Tuttle Creek Lake, Wilson Lake, Waconda Lake, Cedar Bluff Reservoir, Cheney Reservoir, Elk City Lake, John Redmond Reservoir, and Pomona Lake. In addition, dozens of natural lakes and ponds offer Kansans hours of swimming, boating, and fishing enjoyment.

Prairie chickens (right) and butterflies (above) are among
the many kinds of wildlife that flourish in Kansas.

WILDLIFE

Millions of buffalo, or American bison, once roamed the Kansas
prairies. As late as 1871, Major Richard Irving Dodge reported
seeing one huge herd that "was about five days passing a given
point, or not less than 50 miles deep." Sadly, only a few hundred
of these massive beasts survive—on state game preserves—in
Kansas today. Many other kinds of wildlife still flourish, however.
At night, the howling of a coyote still sometimes awakens Kansas
farmers. Deer, antelope, beavers, raccoons, muskrats, skunks,
rabbits, and an occasional bobcat all live in their natural habitats
in Kansas marshes, woods, and prairies. The state boasts the
largest population of prairie chickens in North America, while
pheasant and quail are also common. More than three hundred
species of birds, including the state bird—the western
meadowlark—fill the Kansas sky with life and color.

The Kansas landscape is brightened by such wild plants as cat's-claw (above).

Bluestem, grama, and buffalo grasses grow thickly on the prairie lands that still cover about one-third of the state. So many bright yellow sunflowers rise up in fields and hedgerows that Kansans long ago chose the sunflower as their state flower. Among the many other colorful flowers found in Kansas's grasslands are prairie phlox, ragwort, verbena, and primrose. In drier areas, yucca plant, thistle, and Russian thistle (tumbleweed) are common. Along riverbanks, the leafy branches of willows and cottonwoods rustle with every breeze. Other trees, such as dogwoods, wild plums, walnuts, elms, and sycamores, grow in nearby woods.

CLIMATE

"They used to say that if it wasn't for the wind, when a farmer went out to open his mailbox on a summer afternoon he'd have to

A thunderstorm near Liberal

use a pot holder," joked Pratt County banker Howard K. Loomis
about Kansas heat. In general, however, the state enjoys a
moderate climate, with an average annual temperature of 55
degrees Fahrenheit (13 degrees Celsius). Kansas temperatures
range from near freezing in January to about 80 degrees
Fahrenheit (27 degrees Celsius) in July. When hot, dry air masses
blow up from Mexico or frigid polar winds push down from the
North, they can create very unusual weather conditions.
Thermometers bubbled to a state high of 121 degrees Fahrenheit
(49 degrees Celsius) at Fredonia on July 18, 1936. A record cold
temperature of minus 40 degrees Fahrenheit (minus 40 degrees
Celsius) kept Kansans huddled indoors at Lebanon on
February 13, 1905.

The sun shines more than 275 days each year in Kansas. An
average of about 27 inches (69 centimeters) of moisture wets the
Kansas soil each year. The eastern part of the state receives about
twice as much precipitation as the more arid western counties.
From time to time, great torrents of rain cause streams and rivers
to flood suddenly. Long spells of drought can also occur.

Winter in Butler County

When howling snowstorms sweep into Kansas, their fury can halt all business. A visiting Idaho couple, Nellie and Orville Obendorf, made national news during a blizzard in April 1987. Roof-high snowdrifts kept the couple trapped in their car near Norton, Kansas, for thirteen days before help finally arrived. Even more frightening are the great, funnel-shaped tornadoes that rage through the state on occasion. Sucking up everything in their paths, these swirling storms have killed hundreds of people and destroyed millions of dollars' worth of property. A tornado that hit Topeka in 1966 was perhaps the worst in American history in terms of financial loss. More than half the "twisters" in Kansas have struck in May and June, and when storms approach during tornado season, many farm families run to take refuge in the "cyclone cellars" they have dug into the ground. The 1939 movie *The Wizard of Oz* made Kansas and its tornadoes famous forever. Swept up by a tornado, young Dorothy Gale is dropped into the fantasy land of Oz. After many exciting adventures, she is able to return to Kansas, and realizes joyfully, "There's no place like home."

Chapter 3
THE PEOPLE

THE PEOPLE

*In the country town we gain in contact with our
neighbors. We know people by the score, by the
hundred . . . Our affairs become common with one
another, our joys mutual, and even our sorrows are
shared. . . . It all makes life pleasantly livable.*
—famed Emporia newspaperman William Allen White

According to the 1980 census, 2,364,236 people live in Kansas,
ranking it thirty-second among the states in population. Kansas
continues to grow slowly, and social scientists estimate that the
population will reach 2.5 million by the year 2000. The population
density of the United States as a whole averages 67 people per
square mile (26 people per square kilometer). In comparison,
Kansas remains uncrowded, with an average density of 29 persons
per square mile (11 persons per square kilometer).

Young people searching for jobs have caused shifts in
population from county to county in recent years. In 1920, only
35 percent of Kansans lived in urban areas. Today, 66 percent of
the population have made their homes in cities and towns.
Wichita is the largest city in Kansas, with a population of 279,835.
Other bustling cities in the state are Kansas City, Topeka (the state
capital), Overland Park, Lawrence, Salina, Hutchinson, Olathe,
Leavenworth, and Manhattan.

Although Kansas has changed greatly since newspaperman
William Allen White died in 1944, the emotional comforts of
small-town living seem to thrive even in the cities. In 1984,
Lawrence Mayor David Longhurst remarked that the Kansas way

Graduation day at Haskell Indian Junior College in Lawrence

of life still included "spending time with one's family, playing ball in the park, hearing the laughter of children, living in a community where people care about each other and [say] hello to a stranger."

WHO ARE THE KANSANS?

"I am . . . for opening these lands for the landless of every nation under heaven," stated Kansas Senator Samuel Pomeroy in the early 1860s. "I care not whether he comes to us from the populous cities of our older states, or from the enlightened though oppressed nations of Europe. . . . To me he is an American." The great majority of people living in Kansas today are of Anglo-Saxon heritage. Their American ancestors migrated, in search of opportunity, to Kansas from other states.

Significant numbers of Europeans also settled in Kansas, however, and left their imprint upon the state. As early as 1869, Scandinavians from Norway, Sweden, and Denmark began establishing colonies in Republic, Riley, Cloud, Clay, and Lincoln counties. German-Russians of the peaceful religious sect known as the Mennonites arrived in large numbers during the 1870s. Their farm plows cut the sod as they claimed lands in Marion, McPherson, Harvey, Reno, and other counties. People from the Bohemian region of present-day Czechoslovakia made their way to Kansas, too, and Italians and Yugoslavians found work in the mining region of southeastern Kansas.

Following the Civil War, thousands of former slaves traveled to Kansas to start new lives. Today, more than 128,000 blacks count themselves among the state's citizens. Kickapoo, Sauk, Fox, Iowa, and Pottawatomie Indians still live on reservations in Brown, Doniphan, and Jackson counties. The state's Native American (American Indian) population numbers more than 15,000. Nearly 50,000 Hispanic Americans live in the state today, and Asian immigrants are beginning to join the Kansas labor force.

Religion plays a role in the lives of most Kansans. The state is largely Protestant, with Methodists, Disciples of Christ, Baptists, Presbyterians, Episcopalians, and Lutherans being among the most common Protestant denominations. Roman Catholics make up the largest single religious group in the state. The state also has small numbers of those who follow the Amish, Mennonite, Eastern Orthodox, Dunkard Brethren, and Jewish religions.

REGIONALISM

''You are now entering Kansas, or some state very much like it,'' reads a highway sign depicted in a *New Yorker* magazine cartoon. For years, Americans have joked about Kansas. They think of the state as flat, featureless, and located in the middle of nowhere. They wrongly assume that most Kansans are farmers. These stereotypes, however, fail to give a true picture of Kansas and its people.

Individualism, resourcefulness, vigor, and optimism are

qualities characteristic of the people of Kansas. Manufacturers, doctors, lawyers, bankers, merchants, artists, educators, and other professionals take their place beside Kansas's fabled farmers in making the state great. The challenges of Kansas's rough terrain and turbulent history have bred a spirit of self-reliance, tempered by calm good humor, that is uniquely Kansan. Vince Gibson, well-traveled former football coach of Kansas State University, once stated, ''Let me tell you, Kansas people are the most down-to-earth and the most genuine people I've ever met. They don't know what it is to be phony.''

Those who have an image of Kansas as one vast prairie are uninformed about its varied geography. In fact, the sense of regionalism that can be felt in the state is based partly on the topographical differences between eastern and western Kansas. Most Kansans live in the eastern half of the state, where its largest cities, industries, and mining centers are located. The tall grasses of the Flint Hills support much cattle and dairy production. Elsewhere in the east, black soil has blessed farmers with healthy crops for many years.

West of a north-south line that passes through Salina and Wichita, however, Kansas changes greatly. On the rising western plains, tall grasses give way to short prairie grass. Farmers seated on tractors gaze at the sky in search of needed rain, and winds blow unhindered across the open land. The western third of the state has a true western and southwestern flavor that is more akin to West Texas, New Mexico, or Colorado, than to the Midwest.

Whether Kansans have chosen to live in the eastern or western part of their state, through their hard work they have made it a place of which they can be proud. Kansas is ''the core and kernel of the country,'' remarked former Senator John J. Ingalls in 1896, and those who know the state and its people agree.

Chapter 4
THE FIRST KANSANS

THE FIRST KANSANS

THE EARLIEST NATIVES

Archaeologists near Bonner Springs dug excitedly along the
Kansas River in the spring of 1988. In the gravel they uncovered
ancient arm bones, leg bones, and pieces of human skulls.
"One bone fragment is older than any other previously found in
the New World," exclaimed Kansas geologist Wakefield Dort soon
after scientific testing was done on the bones. The amazing Bonner
Springs discovery proved that people lived in the Kansas region at
least as early as fifteen thousand years ago.

Pottery shards, grindstones, and flint knives are among the
artifacts left by the hunters and gatherers who first wandered the
region. Around A.D. 1000, these people learned basic farming
methods and established villages with simple earthen or clay
dwellings. Near Edwardsville are unusual mounds of piled dirt
that stand 5 feet (1.5 meters) high and measure 25 feet
(8 meters) in diameter. Archaeologists say that these mounds may
have been used in ancient burial ceremonies.

CORONADO'S SEARCH FOR QUIVIRA

High on horseback, their breastplates shining in the sunlight,
the band of soldiers rode northward from Mexico. In 1540,
Spanish *conquistador* Francisco Vásquez de Coronado searched in
vain for the fabled wealth of the Seven Cities of Cíbola. In the

spring of 1541, after wintering in the Rio Grande Valley, the expedition continued northward. They were spurred on by an Indian slave's description of a northern kingdom called "Quivira," whose streets were supposedly paved with gold. For weeks, Coronado's force of thirty men journeyed across vast barren plains. In early June, the soldiers crossed into Kansas near the present-day town of Liberal.

On June 29, 1541, the explorers reached the Arkansas River, east of present-day Dodge City, without yet finding Quivira. "We crossed . . . and went up the other side," wrote one of Coronado's soldiers, "[and] after marching three days we found some Indians who were going hunting." Traveling on the plains among the Quivira (or Wichita) Indians, Coronado in time realized that no city of gold existed. At a hill now called Coronado Heights, just north of Lindsborg in McPherson County, the frustrated explorer finally turned his weary men back toward Mexico in August 1541.

"These provinces," the explorer later wrote, "are a very small affair . . . there is not any gold, nor any metal at all in the country." Still, Coronado claimed the fertile plains for Spain. A priest with the expedition, Juan de Padilla, stayed among the Wichita Indians and performed months of successful Christian missionary work. When the Catholic priest ventured into unfamiliar territory, however, a hostile group of Indians murdered him. He became the first Christian martyr in what is now the United States.

INDIANS OF THE PLAINS

Several Indian groups occupied the Kansas region at the time of the first Spanish exploration. In the northeast lived the Kansa (also called the Kaw), while the Osage claimed lands farther to the

Above: Kansa Chief White Plume
Right: a Pawnee hide painting showing
mounted Pawnees defending themselves
against a raid by Kansa warriors

south. The Wichita still roamed the central region, while the
Pawnee, a powerful, warlike group, gradually advanced from the
north. The men of these various groups hunted buffalo, deer, and
antelope with spears and arrows. The women collected nuts and
berries in woven baskets and tended rows of corn and pumpkins.
From animal skins and bones the Indians fashioned clothing,
tools, and wall coverings for their tepee shelters. In western
Kansas, a group of Picuris Indians lived for a time. The remnants
of one of their unusual stone and adobe dwellings, known as "El
Cuartelejo," still stands in Scott County.

Contact with the Spanish who settled as far north as New
Mexico dramatically changed Indian life on the Great Plains.
Indian raiders galloped northward on stolen Spanish horses. Able
to travel greater distances on horseback, Comanche, Kiowa,
Cheyenne, and Arapaho Indians all pushed into western Kansas

by the 1800s. The Indians of the plains preferred the lifestyle of the nomad to that of farming. Hunters on horseback chased down buffalo, and when the buffalo herds migrated, the Indians packed their belongings and followed them. When rival groups sought to occupy the same lands, violent Indian wars broke out. The savage Comanche in particular gained a reputation as fearsome warriors.

THE LOUISIANA PURCHASE

Canoe paddles gently cut the surface of the water as French explorers Jacques Marquette and Louis Jolliet first explored the mighty Mississippi River in 1673. During the next decades, other curious Frenchmen left the Great Lakes region and ventured up the rivers flowing east from Kansas. Charles Claude du Tisne journeyed up the Missouri River in 1719 and encountered both Osage and Pawnee Indians. To drive the encroaching French from the plains, a Spanish force of forty-two soldiers commanded by Don Pedro de Villasur soon marched north from Santa Fe, New Mexico. The Spanish clashed with Pawnee warriors just north of the Platte River in Nebraska. Few of the stunned and bloodied soldiers managed to escape. Taking advantage of the Spanish defeat, the French soon made greater claims upon the Kansas region.

Étienne de Bourgmont explored as far west as present-day Saline and Ellsworth counties in 1724. Paul and Pierre Mallet crossed the plains all the way from the Platte River to Santa Fe in 1739. In 1744, French fur trappers built a log stockade, called Fort Cavagnial, near present-day Leavenworth. It was used as a trading post for nearly twenty years.

In 1763, as part of the treaty ending the French and Indian War, France ceded to Spain the entire Louisiana country, which included the Kansas region. French traders remained influential, however, and with the Treaty of San Ildefonso in 1800, France regained control of the vast Louisiana wilderness. In Europe, French Emperor Napoleon Bonaparte was expecting war with England. To finance his army, Napoleon offered to sell all of Louisiana to the United States. In 1803, President Thomas Jefferson gladly paid the price of $15 million. The purchase of Louisiana instantly doubled the size of the United States. The Kansas region had become American.

AMERICAN EXPLORERS

President Jefferson sent a party of forty-five soldiers and pioneers westward to examine America's new Louisiana Purchase lands. Commanded by Meriwether Lewis and William Clark, this "Corps of Discovery" left St. Louis on May 14, 1804.

On June 26, the hardy explorers camped at the junction of the Kansas and Missouri rivers. "On all sides the country is fine," Lewis and Clark penned in their journal as they sailed in keelboats farther up the Missouri River. The adventurers saw two Kansa Indian villages along the riverbank before passing beyond the present-day boundary of Kansas on July 12. During the next two years, the expedition crossed the Rocky Mountains, reached the shore of the Pacific Ocean, and made the difficult journey eastward again. On September 15, 1806, the men had recrossed the Great Plains and were camped once more at the mouth of the Kansas River. "The low grounds are now delightful," recorded Lewis and Clark, "and the whole country exhibits a rich appearance." By September 23, Lewis and Clark were back in St. Louis, and Americans marveled at the stories of their great adventure.

Lieutenant Zebulon M. Pike led another major expedition west in 1806. During August and September, Pike's party rode across the Kansas region. Sitting at separate council meetings with the Kansa, Osage, and Pawnee, Pike offered the Indians peace under the American flag. Pike then journeyed farther west along the Smoky Hill, Saline, and Solomon rivers. He and two of his men traveled as far as the Rocky Mountains and sighted the great snowy peak that bears his name today. When he returned to civilization, Pike described his season in the western Kansas region. "In that vast country of which I speak, we find soil generally dry and sandy. . . . These vast plains . . . may become in time as celebrated as the sandy deserts of Africa."

Major Stephen H. Long stood on the deck of the steamboat *Western Engineer* as it churned its way up the Missouri River in 1819. Of the Kansas countryside he wrote, "Its valley . . . has a deep and fertile soil, bearing similar forests of cotton-wood, sycamore, & interspersed with meadow; but in ascending trees become more and more scattered, and at length disappear almost entirely, the country, at its source, being one immense prairie." Traveling overland across the barren, open plains, Long was clearly disappointed with the land. On maps he later misleadingly labeled the prairie "The Great American Desert."

THE SANTA FE TRAIL

Despite Pike's and Long's less than favorable reports about the land, dozens of hopeful American trappers and traders began crossing the Kansas region. In September 1821, Captain William Becknell led seventeen men from Franklin, Missouri, into the Kansas wilderness. Leading strings of pack mules, the traders crossed the Arkansas River and pushed southwest across the

The Last Chance Store (right) was the last supply stop for those traveling
along the Santa Fe Trail, which still bears ruts made by wagon wheels (left).

rolling plains toward the Mexican town of Santa Fe. At last, in
mid-September, the dusty men reached their destination. There
they traded their cloth, buttons, pans, and other goods for a huge
profit in silver and furs. The next year, Becknell made a second
trip to Santa Fe using wagons along his established trail. When
other Missouri traders saw his saddlebags brimming with
Mexican gold and silver, they, too, followed along the winding
Santa Fe Trail.

At a place aptly named Council Grove, in east-central Kansas,
United States government commissioners and Osage chieftains
met in 1825. Together they signed a treaty guaranteeing peaceful
travel along the trail. Soon a survey team mapped the trail, two-
thirds of which was located in present-day Kansas. Over the next
forty years, trading along the Santa Fe Trail thrived. After 1829,
Fort Leavenworth became the starting point for all military
caravans taking the trail.

INDIANS IN A FOREIGN LAND

During the 1820s and 1830s, a great tide of land-hungry pioneers pushed west toward the Mississippi River. The United States government, after conquering the Indians of the Ohio River Valley and the Great Lakes region, sought to clear them from the area forever. Through peaceful treaties with Kansa and Osage chiefs, the government obtained huge tracts of Kansas land on which to settle the defeated Indians from the East. Beginning in 1829, during forced removals, nearly thirty different native groups trudged west and crossed the Missouri River into the "Indian Country" of eastern Kansas. Included were such groups as the Shawnee, Delaware, Wyandot, Miami, Ottawa, Pottawatomie, Kickapoo, Chippewa, Iowa, Sac, and Fox. One narrow strip of land along the southern border of the territory was reserved for the Cherokee Indians.

The upheaval caused much suffering among the Indians. The agent who traveled with one group of Ottawa, for example, reported, "Out of about 600 emigrants, more than 300 died within the first two years, because of exposure, lack of proper food, and the great difference between the cool, damp woods of Ohio and the dry, hot plains of Kansas."

Daniel Morgan Boone, son of famed explorer Daniel Boone, lived among the Kansa Indians after 1827 in present-day Jefferson County, teaching them farming methods. Other white men also tried to help the Indians adapt. The Reverend Thomas Johnson opened the Shawnee Methodist Mission near Turner in present-day Wyandotte County in 1830. He later moved it to Johnson County. Kindly Baptist preacher Isaac McCoy established a number of missions and schools for Indians in Kansas, including the Shawnee Baptist Mission in 1831. In 1833, the Reverend

Jotham Meeker arrived at that mission, bringing with him the first printing press to be used in Kansas. On February 24, 1835, Meeker published the first issue of the *Shawnee Sun* (*Siwinowe Kesibwi*), a newspaper in the Shawnee language. Missions established by the Quakers, Presbyterians, Roman Catholics, and other religious groups also aided the Indians. Even so, disease and hardship killed many of these transplanted Native Americans. Others plowed fields and planted crops and orchards, successfully learning white farming methods in their strange new homeland.

THE KANSAS TERRITORY

ROAD TO OREGON read the sign posted near present-day Gardner about 40 miles (64 kilometers) along the Santa Fe Trail. On a route that branched off from the Santa Fe Trail, settlers headed northwest to the fertile lands of the distant Oregon Territory. Seated on great ox-drawn wagons called "prairie schooners," thousands of people traveled along the Oregon Trail during the 1840s, crossing out of the Kansas region beyond the Blue River near Marysville. Plains Indians named the trail the "White-Topped Wagon Road." The discovery of gold in California in 1848 increased the flood of traffic as "forty-niners" rushed to seek their fortunes there.

America's final victory in the Mexican War in 1848 won the New Mexico region for the United States. As a result, even more traders traveled the Santa Fe Trail. Such military outposts in Kansas as Fort Riley and Fort Larned helped protect travelers from attacks by angry Indians. Kansas settlement increased as word spread that the treeless prairies offered fine farming possibilities. In 1853, the United States government forced a number of Indian groups to accept revisions to their treaties. As a

Fort Larned was built in 1859 to protect travelers on the Santa Fe Trail.

result, more than 13 million acres (5.3 million hectares) of Kansas land that had been promised to the Indians "forever" were instantly reclaimed by the United States. Within twenty-five years, nearly all the Indians living in Kansas were forced southward into Indian Territory (present-day Oklahoma).

During the early months of 1854, congressmen in Washington debated loudly over how the Great Plains region should be developed. The Missouri Compromise of 1820 had guaranteed that no slavery would ever be allowed north of Missouri's southern boundary. Anxious to maintain a balance of power in Congress, politicians from the southern slaveholding states insisted on a new law. Finally, Illinois Senator Stephen Douglas offered a bill creating two new territories, Kansas and Nebraska. Using a method called "popular sovereignty," the settlers in the two territories would vote and decide whether or not to allow slavery. On May 30, 1854, President Franklin Pierce signed the Kansas-Nebraska Act, which created the Kansas Territory. Its boundaries

Proslavery Missourians murdered five free-state Kansans during the 1858
Marais des Cygnes massacre.

were those of present-day Kansas along the north, south, and
eastern borders, while to the west the territory stretched as far as
the foothills of the Rocky Mountains.

BLEEDING KANSAS

Suddenly, it seemed, all Americans turned their eyes toward
Kansas. Northern abolitionists (those who wanted to end slavery)
vowed to keep slavery out of the territory, while southerners
demanded that Kansas become a slave state. The destiny of Kansas
depended upon its settlers. In Massachusetts, Eli Thayer, Amos
Lawrence, and others formed the New England Emigrant Aid
Society and hurriedly sent homesteaders west to make Kansas a
free state. When they arrived, they founded such towns as Topeka
and Lawrence. Other northern groups sent organized parties west

as well. Members of minister Henry Ward Beecher's New York church provided "free-state" settlers with Sharps carbines with which to protect themselves. These rifles came to be called "Beecher's Bibles."

Angry southerners urged quick settlement of Kansas by "slave-staters." "[You] know how to protect your interests," roared Missouri Senator David Atchison, "your rifles will free you from such neighbors. . . . You will go there, if necessary with the *bayonet* and *blood*!" Soon hundreds of "Border Ruffians" rushed into Kansas from nearby Missouri to take control of the territory. They passed illegal "Bogus Laws" that protected slavery in Kansas.

Tensions rose, tempers flared, and violence soon broke out. When a free-state man was murdered in November 1855, fiery free-stater James Lane raised an army of vengeful militiamen. In what became known as the "Wakarusa War," these troops paraded in a show of force for a few weeks outside Lawrence. Then, on May 21, 1856, some eight hundred mounted Border Ruffians suddenly swooped down on Lawrence, burning buildings and destroying the property of free-staters.

The infamous sacking of Lawrence caused one free-stater, in particular, to rage with fury. Fifty-six-year-old John Brown impressed everyone who met him. "He was somewhat tall, gaunt, erect and soldierly in appearance with . . . grey hair, full beard . . . and a keen grey eye that once seen was never forgotten," recalled Kansan L. D. Bailey. At midnight on May 23, Brown and seven followers dragged five proslavery settlers from their cabins along Pottawatomie Creek and without mercy hacked them to death with swords. Before leaving Kansas in 1859, Brown commanded abolitionists in clashes with slave-staters at the Battle of Black Jack near Baldwin and at Osawatomie. In October 1859, Brown led a bloody attack on the federal arsenal at Harpers Ferry,

Though the covered wagon (above) was the usual method of travel across Kansas, some inventive travelers devised "wind wagons" (left).

Virginia, in a mad attempt to free all slaves. Hung for his crimes, John Brown became a national legend in the fight against slavery.

At the same time, other Kansas clashes occurred between free-staters and slave-staters at such places as Franklin; Hickory Point, near Oskaloosa; and the Marais des Cygnes River, where five free-staters were massacred. Free-staters calling themselves "Jayhawkers," after a mythical plundering bird, conducted raids upon Border Ruffian strongholds across the border in Missouri. Slaves brought back from Missouri were kept safe at secret houses in Topeka and Lawrence while traveling north to freedom on the "Underground Railroad." Between 1854 and 1861, some two hundred people died trying to determine the future of Kansas. Their efforts won the territory the unforgettable nickname Bleeding Kansas.

NEW TRAILS ACROSS THE PLAINS

"The gold fever is raging in every town in Kansas," exclaimed the Atchison newspaper *Freedom's Champion* in 1858. Word of gold discoveries in the Pikes Peak and Denver areas of the Rockies sent fortune hunters rushing west across Kansas. During the next year, miners cut dusty new trails across the territory. Some proudly painted the words PIKES PEAK OR BUST on their covered wagons. A few inventive travelers hammered together "wind wagons." The wind filled the sails of these strange vehicles and sped them forward like boats sailing over a rolling ocean of grass.

Western miners provided business for freight and stagecoach lines. The Butterfield Overland Despatch Company, for example, began carrying mail to California along the Smoky Hill River in 1865. Travelers and teamsters wheeling along the Leavenworth & Pikes Peak Express to Denver stopped at nineteen Kansas way stations during their long journeys.

"Great Express Enterprise! . . . Clear the Track and Let the Pony Come Through!" cried the Leavenworth *Daily Times* in April 1860. The fabulous Pony Express raced mail riders across plains and mountains the 2,000 miles (3,219 kilometers) from St. Joseph, Missouri, to Sacramento, California, in just ten days. "The pony-rider was usually a little bit of a man, brimful of spirit and endurance," marveled famed writer Mark Twain. Express riders traveled light and stopped at stations every 10 miles (16 kilometers) in order to jump onto a fresh horse. A letter sent by Pony Express cost the sender five dollars. The Pony Express route crossed northeastern Kansas through Doniphan, Brown, Nemaha, Marshall, and Washington counties before passing into Nebraska. Bouncing along by stagecoach to Nevada, Mark Twain once spied one rider. "Away across the endless dead level of the prairie a black speck appears against the sky. . . . In a second or two it becomes a horse and rider, rising and falling, rising and falling . . . a whoop and a hurrah from our upper deck, a wave of the rider's hand . . . and man and horse burst past our excited faces, and go swinging away like a belated fragment of a storm!"

The Pony Express thrilled Americans for eighteen months. The unprofitable enterprise ended in the fall of 1861, however, after telegraph workers finished stringing the first transcontinental wire.

THE BATTLE FOR STATEHOOD

We cross the prairies as of old
The pilgrims crossed the sea,
To make the West, as they the East,
The homestead of the free.
  —from "The Kansas Emigrant's
  Song" by John Greenleaf Whittier

While Jayhawkers and Border Ruffians skirmished violently, the difficult task of making Kansas a state remained. In seven years, ten men served as territorial governor—and all ruled with little success. At two separate conventions, at Topeka in 1855 and at Lecompton in 1857, territorial delegates wrote state constitutions, but after heated debates, Congress rejected each of them.

In time, southerners learned that the traditional slave crops of cotton and tobacco grew poorly in the dry Kansas climate. Consequently, despite the bloody fighting, slavery never took hold in Kansas. Northern settlers continued to come to the territory, however. With sweat and toil, they plowed plots of land and built themselves crude cabins. While traveling through Kansas in 1859, famed newspaper editor Horace Greeley observed wryly, "It takes three log houses to make a city in Kansas, but they begin *calling* it a city so soon as they have staked out the lots." A terrible drought during 1859 ruined crops and thousands of starving settlers fled back East. Still, enough hardy homesteaders remained for Kansas to qualify for statehood.

A statue in Marysville honors the Pony Express, which crossed through northeastern Kansas.

Finally, in July 1859, delegates gathered at Wyandotte (now part of Kansas City) to frame yet another constitution. Their document prohibited slavery in Kansas and fixed the western boundary where it stands today. For years, the name of the region had been spelled more than fifty different ways, including "Canzas," "Kansez," and "Konza," but the delegates chose "Kansas" as the official spelling of the name of their state.

The southern members of Congress bitterly opposed this constitution, but in 1861, before it was voted on, the southern states began withdrawing from the Union. The remaining members of Congress approved the constitution. President James Buchanan at last signed Kansas's admission bill into law on January 29, 1861. Citizens across the new state shouted in celebration as Kansas became the thirty-fourth star on the United States flag.

Chapter 5
TAMING THE PLAINS

TAMING THE PLAINS

THE PROOF OF PATRIOTISM

As Kansas eagerly joined the Union, eleven discontented southern states chose to leave it. To protect the right to own slaves, they formed the independent Confederate States of America. The American Civil War erupted in April 1861, when Confederate troops bombarded federal Fort Sumter at Charleston, South Carolina. President Abraham Lincoln vowed to hold the United States together and called promptly for loyal volunteers to put down the southern rebellion.

Kansas, though sparsely populated, raised twenty-three army regiments and four artillery batteries during the war. An astonishing total of more than twenty thousand men—two-thirds of the state's adult males—served in the war. Singing the rousing tune "John Brown's Body," most of these soldiers marched off to fight in Missouri and east of the Mississippi River.

Several Kansas towns were raided by Confederate guerrilla units. These irregular soldiers, called "bushwhackers," roared through Humboldt, Gardner, and Olathe in 1861, plundering stores and burning houses. The worst raid occurred on August 21, 1863, when William C. Quantrill led his three hundred bushwhackers rampaging into Lawrence. During the surprise attack, the raiders shot the windows out of homes and stores. Scores of defenseless Lawrence citizens were shot down as they ran for cover. The attackers looted stores, banks, and saloons.

Confederate guerrillas led by William C. Quantrill raided Lawrence in August 1863, killing many citizens and destroying most of the town.

After setting fire to most of the town, Quantrill and his men rode for the Missouri border. Rising from his cellar hiding place, the stunned Reverend H. D. Fisher soon discovered that "more than one hundred and eighty of our citizens had been killed and . . . the whole business part of our town was in ashes."

A regular Confederate army commanded by General Sterling Price threatened to invade eastern Kansas in 1864. Kansas militiamen rushed to join regular Union troops and clashed with Price's forces along the Blue River near the town of Westport, just across the border in Missouri. As the Confederates retreated, the Union troops successfully struck again in Linn County, Kansas. During this Battle of Mine Creek, one Kansas soldier later remembered, "Feds and Confeds were all mixed in a life and death struggle. The roar of musketry, the rattle of rifles and pistols . . . and the shrieks of the wounded, created a scene that was perfectly awful." The Civil War ended in April 1865 with a Union victory. The thousands of toughened veterans who returned to Kansas clearly had done their share to preserve the nation and abolish slavery forever.

EARLY KANSAS GROWTH

"Ad Astra per Aspera" is the Kansas state motto. Its Latin words mean "To the Stars through Difficulties," and Kansas did indeed survive some troubles during its earliest years of statehood. In 1859, after a heated debate, Kansans chose to make Topeka the state capital. "We had nothing with which to set up housekeeping except the State Seal, a lease on some leaky buildings, and quite an assortment of bills payable," confessed early Governor Samuel J. Crawford.

The state's first governor, Charles Robinson, encountered problems right away. Although an impeachment trial found him not guilty of selling state bonds illegally, the scandal ruined his career. Kansas's first two senators met sad fates as well. Senator Jim Lane, the famous Kansas free-soil general, shot himself to death in 1866 when faced with money problems and failing health. In 1873, Senator Samuel C. Pomeroy was forced to retire from politics after he was accused of attempting political bribery.

Edmund G. Ross filled Jim Lane's seat in the U.S. Senate in 1866. Ross soon suffered the disapproval of Kansans simply by staying true to his ideals. As an abolitionist Republican from a staunchly Republican state, Ross was expected to support policies that would take revenge on the defeated South. President Andrew Johnson, however, wished to treat the southerners with more kindness than cruelty. After Johnson vetoed several harsh anti-Southern bills in 1868, Congress tried to impeach him for treason.

During the trial, many people believed the close verdict would hinge on Ross's vote. "I almost literally looked down into my open grave," Ross later remarked. "Friendships, position, fortune . . . were about to be swept away by the breath of my mouth." Ross's crucial vote of "not guilty" saved President Johnson from being removed from office. Unfortunately, it also destroyed Ross's future in Kansas politics. He did, however, go on to serve a four-year term as territorial governor of New Mexico.

While the state's politicians struggled to win public office, many other Kansans fought to tame the land. Thousands of new settlers journeyed to Kansas following the Civil War. "Homesteads are taken, farms are bought, town lots are changing hands. . . . Yes, we are prospering," exclaimed one happy Kansas newspaperman as early as 1863. One reason people went west to Kansas was the promise of free land. The Homestead Act of 1862 offered 160 acres (65 hectares) of federal land to any citizen who paid a ten-dollar filing fee and agreed to live on and improve the property for five years.

In 1873, the Timber Culture Act promised the same amount of land to anyone who would plant one-fourth of it in trees within four years. By that time, hopeful Kansas homesteaders had claimed about 6 million acres (2.4 million hectares), and the state's population had mushroomed to more than 360,000.

THE RAILROADS PUSH WEST

Work crews graded the routes, laid the wooden ties, and pounded the spikes that held the heavy iron rails in place. The first railroad in Kansas, the Elwood and Marysville line, laid 5 miles (8 kilometers) of track from Elwood to Wathena in 1857. To encourage additional railroad building, the federal government

Locomotives such as this were used on the first railroads that snaked through Kansas.

offered land grants to railroad companies. After the Civil War, dozens of companies scrambled for construction rights as railroad fever spread.

Among the early railroads snaking through Kansas were the Leavenworth, Lawrence & Fort Gibson Railroad; the Missouri River, Fort Scott & Gulf Railroad; and the Missouri, Kansas & Texas Railroad, fondly known as the "Katy." The Atchison, Topeka & Santa Fe Railroad stretched along much of the old Santa Fe Trail. During the 1872 construction of this famous railroad, tireless work crews laid 271 miles (436 kilometers) of rail in just 222 days. In 1876, Fred Harvey first offered food service at stops along the Santa Fe line. The crisply uniformed young women who worked in his hotel dining rooms in Florence, Topeka, and elsewhere soon became known as "Harvey Girls."

Another historic railroad, the Union Pacific, Eastern Division (also known as the Kansas Pacific), was begun in 1863. From Lawrence to Topeka to Junction City, the line steadily pushed

Killed by the thousands for their meat and hides (above), the buffalos that once roamed the Kansas prairies had virtually disappeared by the late 1870s.

westward until it finally reached Denver in 1870. More than once, Indians attacked work crews. Blizzards sometimes slowed progress, as well. Even so, the company raced excitedly to finish its task. One outgrowth of this railroad building was the "end of track" town. Towns such as Coyote, Monument, and Sheridan sprang up in succession wherever construction temporarily paused. Railroad workers, tradesmen, and adventure-seekers crowded together in hotels, gambling houses, and saloons.

In all, some two hundred railroad companies laid track across Kansas. By 1880, locomotives belching smoke carried freight and passengers along 3,104 miles (4,995 kilometers) of Kansas railways. Selling land-grant acreage and offering reduced fares to arriving settlers, the railroads helped open the state for development.

THE FATE OF THE INDIANS

Those Indians living in eastern Kansas had been pushed off their lands and forced to move south into Indian Territory before the outbreak of the Civil War. The coming of the railroads in the late 1860s destroyed the way of life of Kansas's western Plains Indians. The Comanche, Kiowa, Arapaho, Cheyenne, and Apache soon discovered hundreds of pioneers settling on their traditional lands. Even worse, hunters roamed the prairies, killing hundreds of thousands of buffalo merely for their hides. William "Buffalo Bill" Cody, while employed by the Union Pacific to provide meat for workers, was said to have killed 4,280 buffalo in eighteen months. Sportsmen slaughtered the animals for pleasure, sometimes shooting the shaggy beasts from the windows of trains.

Outraged at seeing their source of food disappear and their way of life threatened, the Indians fought back, attacking isolated homesteads with terrifying violence. In the 1860s, the United States Army established additional outposts in Kansas, including Forts Harker, Zarah, Hays, Wallace, and Dodge, to protect homesteaders and travelers. In October 1867, some fifteen thousand Indians gathered at Medicine Lodge to discuss peace with United States government commissioners. Speaking for the various Plains Indians, Comanche Chief Ten Bears pleaded, "I was born on the prairie where the wind blew free and there was nothing to break the light of the sun. I was born where there are no enclosures and where everything drew a free breath. I want to die there and not within walls."

Although the Indians agreed to surrender all lands north of the Arkansas River, the bloodshed continued. During 1868 and 1869, two hundred settlers were attacked and killed in Kansas. Some of these raids were probably caused by the invasion of white hunters into the Indian hunting grounds south of the river. In the summer of 1874, Cheyenne bands raided parts of western Kansas.

The last Indian raids in Kansas occurred in September 1878. More than a hundred unhappy, sick, and hungry Northern Cheyenne, led by Chiefs Dull Knife and Little Wolf, left their reservation to return to their home in the north. "The country is filled with Indians," the panicked mayor of Dodge City telegraphed the governor. For two weeks, these raiders cut a bloody path across the state. Finally captured in Nebraska and Montana, the surrender of the Cheyenne ended the long struggle of the Indians to keep their homeland.

THE HARD LIFE OF THE SODBUSTER

Free government land and cheap railroad land enticed thousands of American and European immigrants to journey west to Kansas. Using sturdy plows, these "sodbusters" cut the thick grass of the prairies and planted crops. They shoveled into the ground of the treeless plains and built dugouts in which to live. Cutting up large squares of sod, they fashioned walls and roofs for the portions of their new homes that jutted above the ground. Most settlers on the plains, not having wood, gathered dried buffalo manure and burned these "buffalo chips" for fuel. Farmers also often collected buffalo bones, which they sold to be crushed for fertilizer.

"It is hard work, hard work, I tell you, and little pay," exclaimed one Kansas pioneer woman. In addition to the threat of Indian attack, the farmers faced many other difficulties and dangers. The loneliness of the sparsely populated prairie filled many settlers with despair. Others died of illnesses or injuries, miles away from the nearest doctors. Nature challenged the

An 1880s sod house is preserved at the Thomas County Museum in Colby.

Kansas pioneers constantly. "Rattlesnakes, bedbugs, fleas, and the 'prairie itch' were what kept us awake at nights and made life miserable," remarked Rush County settler W. H. Russell.

Many farmers hardly survived the sudden invasion of a plague of grasshoppers in 1874. Fourteen-year-old Ferdinand Funk of Marion County remembered the day of August 6:

> The sky suddenly became hazy and speedily darkened. . . . Then with a whizzing, whirring sound the grasshoppers came from the northwest and in unbelievable numbers. They lit on everything. I was covered from head to foot. . . . The ground was covered, in some spots to a depth of three or four inches, and trees along the creek were so loaded with grasshoppers that large limbs were broken off.

Eating every plant in sight, the grasshoppers destroyed crops on some 5,000 square miles (12,950 square kilometers) of Kansas farmland.

Taming the plains required a never-ending battle with Kansas weather, as well. Winter blizzards covered dugouts with snow and forced trains to remain stranded on the prairies for days.

This photograph from the late 1800s shows Kansas cowboys congregating at the chuck wagon after a long day of work.

Sudden rainstorms caused rivers and creeks to overflow, flooding croplands and pioneer homes alike. Long droughts caused the greatest fears, however. The blazing sun withered crops and cracked dry riverbeds. Dry grass caught fire easily, and prairie fires were truly frightening. Elizabeth Custer, wife of General George Custer, witnessed one such fire while living at Fort Hays. "As the sky became lurid, and the blaze swept on toward us," she exclaimed, ". . . it seemed that the end of the world . . . had really come. The whole earth appeared to be on fire." Frantic settlers started backfires, furrowed up protective borders of soil, or beat at the approaching flames with wet blankets. Even so, prairie fires often claimed crops, homes, and lives.

CATTLE TRAILS AND COWTOWNS

After the Civil War, millions of native, wild, longhorn cattle ran free in Texas, while in the north, a shortage of beef existed. Texans wisely took advantage of the northern demand by driving their

cattle to the nearest rail connections in Kansas. Two early destinations were Baxter Springs and Coffeyville. In the spring of 1867, however, Illinois livestock dealer Joseph McCoy chose the new Union Pacific railroad town of Abilene as the best cattle-shipping location. He promptly built a stockyard, corrals, and a hotel and eagerly advertised for business. By year's end, McCoy had successfully shipped thirty-five thousand longhorns to eastern markets.

Each spring and summer, lean and sturdy Texas cowboys wearing broad-brimmed hats, chaps, and kerchiefs headed their "dogies" northward across Indian Territory to Kansas. The first important trail to Kansas was the Chisholm Trail, a route earlier blazed by Wichita trader Jesse Chisholm. Along the way, the cattle fattened themselves by grazing on prairie grasses. When the animals remained calm, cattle-driving could be pleasant. Sudden panics, however, sent herds stampeding madly. At those times, cowboys whipped their horses into a gallop and risked their lives to regain control of the cattle.

As both the Union Pacific and the Atchison, Topeka & Santa Fe railroads pushed farther westward, a new cowtown took the place

Dodge City, which thrived from 1875 to 1885, was the greatest of the Kansas cowtowns.

of a former one. Newton, Ellsworth, Wichita, Hunnewell, and Caldwell all served as important shipping points for a time. Beginning in 1875, Dodge City thrived a full ten years, longer than any other cowtown.

The Kansas cowtowns gave birth to many of the legends of the Wild West. After long cattle drives, cowboys crowded into cowtown saloons, dance halls, and gambling dens to spend their hard-earned pay. Drunken brawls and blasting six-shooters made life dangerous for average citizens. In 1871, to combat lawlessness, the people of Abilene hired James Butler "Wild Bill" Hickok, the former peace officer of Hays. Hickok's fearsome reputation as a gunman soon quieted Abilene, and he spent much of his time playing cards at the Alamo saloon during his eight months as town marshal.

A number of Dodge City gunfighters and peace officers gained fame over the years. Wyatt Earp, Bat Masterson, Doc Holliday,

Wild Bill Hickok (above) tamed the cowtown of Abilene. The Dodge City Peace Commission (left) included such famous lawmen as Bat Masterson, Charlie Bassett, and Wyatt Earp.

Charlie Bassett, and Luke Short all walked the dusty streets of Dodge and drank whiskey at the famous Long Branch Saloon. As many as forty men died of gunshot wounds in the Kansas cowtowns between 1870 and 1885. But as the era of cattle drives reached its end, calm returned to the Kansas prairies.

BOOMS AND BUSTS

By the late 1870s, cattle-ranching associations such as the Comanche Cattle Pool controlled much of Kansas's open range, while farmers strung barbed wire along the edges of their property. Good weather and improved farming methods attracted droves of new settlers to Kansas. In 1873, for example, wealthy Scot George Grant bought more than 25,000 acres (10,117 hectares) in Ellis County and established the town of Victoria. In the 1880s, Englishman F. J. S. Turnly bought 17,000 acres (6,880 hectares) in

Harper County and founded the farming village of Runnymede. Europeans streamed into the state, and groups of Americans formed colonies, as well. In the 1870s, some fifteen thousand former slaves made their way from the South to Kansas, settling in such communities as Nicodemus in Graham County.

Kansas railroads extended their lines and services to make all regions of the state accessible. Land developers saw opportunities and quickly seized them. Albert Warren and James Keeney, for example, founded WaKeeney in Trego County and successfully advertised lots for sale in the Chicago newspapers. Other speculators promoted such instant towns as Hodgeman Center, Lakin, Kalvesta, Nonchalanta, and Ness City. "All roads lead to Ravanna—Gaze on the Map and See For Yourselves" read a printed sales pitch for that town. Great irrigation projects along the Arkansas River intensified interest in western Kansas lands. Miles of ditches and canals stretching from Garden City southeast to Dodge City attracted a rush of settlers in the 1880s. During these boom years, homesteaders lined up at land offices for days, waiting excitedly for a chance to file claims.

Repeated summer droughts and winter storms quickly turned the Kansas boom into a bust by 1887. The cruel blizzard of 1886 alone killed fully 20 percent of the state's cattle herds. With each failing season, farmers faced greater troubles and deeper debts. "In God We Trusted, In Kansas We Busted," joked settlers grimly as they were forced to leave. As the state fell into a depression, Senator John J. Ingalls observed sadly, "Empty railroad trains ran across deserted prairies to vacant towns."

Crop prices fell drastically. Kansas wheat dropped in value from $1.19 a bushel in 1881 to just 49¢ in 1890. Some desperate Kansans joined those who, on September 16, 1893, rushed south to grab up new lands opening up in Oklahoma. Those settlers

Dunlap, which had its own school (left), was one of several Kansas communities settled by blacks in the late 1800s.

determined to stay in Kansas recognized quickly that county seats drew more business than other towns. In the late 1880s, towns in several new Kansas counties fought violently to win the honor of being named county seat. Double sets of county officers, charges of voting fraud, and bloodshed marked the struggle for county seats in more than twenty counties. When Leoti and Coronado were competing to become county seat of Wichita County, for example, three men were killed and seven others were badly wounded. The "County-Seat Wars" resulted in much bitterness among western Kansas citizens.

POPULISM AND PROHIBITIONISM

Kansas farmers struggling in the late 1880s often felt like victims. Banks held mortgages on many farms. Railroad owners

Orator Mary Lease (above) and politicians William Peffer and Jerry Simpson (depicted at right on the cover of a popular humor magazine) were among a number of noted Kansans who championed Populism.

charged unfair rates to ship farm produce to market. In frustration, Kansans formed the Farmers' Alliance. In 1890, the group helped create the People's (or Populist) party, a national political party.

"Wealth belongs to him who creates it," proclaimed Populist pamphlets as the party spread its influence throughout the plains and western states. In Kansas, Populist "revivalists" crusaded from town to town giving fiery speeches. One speaker, Mrs. Mary "Yellin' " Lease, won national fame as the "Lady Orator of the West." To fight Wall Street's powerful financial interests, she urged her farmer audiences to "raise less corn and more Hell!"

While running for Congress in 1890, Populist Jeremiah Simpson of Medicine Lodge exclaimed that his princely Republican opponent wore silk stockings while he, Simpson, had none. That fall, Kansas voters successfully sent "Sockless Jerry" Simpson to Washington, D.C. During the early 1890s, many other Populists also won political office in Kansas. Bitterly contested state races in 1892 resulted in many Populists and Republicans claiming the same seats in the statehouse. Amid shouts and fistfights, state militiamen marched into the capitol to restore order when the legislature met in 1893. During their time in power, Kansas's Populists enacted state laws that more fairly regulated banks, stockyards, railroads, telegraph companies, and building-and-loan associations. A new ballot law made voting easier and guarded against corruption. At last the voice of the farmer was being heard in Kansas.

Years earlier, another social movement had helped make Kansas unique. Members of the Women's Christian Temperance Union and other organizations had long urged that liquor be outlawed in the state. In 1879, Governor John St. John offered a prohibition amendment to the state constitution. Kansans passed it into law by eight thousand votes. Consequently, in 1880, Kansas became the first state in the Union to go "dry."

While prohibitionists rejoiced, Kansans still found ways to get a drink. Illegal saloons were run in some of the back rooms of stores. Kansas druggists, permitted to sell alcohol for medicinal purposes, often proved generous in filling requests. Through the years, prohibitionists voiced outrage at this lawbreaking. In 1900, one woman, Carry Nation, began attempting to enforce the law herself. In Kiowa, Wichita, Enterprise, and other towns, she entered saloons swinging a hatchet and hurling rocks. Carry Nation's famed crusade shut down a number of illegal bars. Yet for many years to follow, Kansans argued heatedly about their prohibition law.

Chapter 6
THE RISE OF
MODERN KANSAS

THE RISE OF MODERN KANSAS

THE SPIRIT OF PROGRESS

On October 5, 1892, the notorious Dalton Gang galloped into
Coffeyville. The five bandits robbed the town's two banks and
then attempted to escape, but Coffeyville citizens grabbed their
rifles and fought back. Bullets whistled, blood spilled into the
streets, and within minutes, four of the robbers were dead and the
fifth man, Emmett Dalton, lay seriously wounded. It can be said
that the defeat of the Dalton Gang signaled the end of the Wild
West in Kansas.

By the late 1890s, Populism was fading in Kansas. The economy
faltered under Populist government, and Kansas citizens went to
other states in search of opportunities. "What's the Matter with
Kansas?" asked William Allen White, the young editor of the
Emporia *Gazette*, in 1896. "Go East and you hear them laugh at
Kansas, go West and they sneer at her, go South and they 'cuss'
her, go North and they have forgotten her." White's provocative
editorial brought him nationwide fame. As a member of the
Progressive branch of the Republican party, he urged a new spirit
of progress in the state.

During the Progressive administrations of governors Edward
Hoch and Walter R. Stubbs, from 1905 to 1913, many new reform
laws filled Kansans with hope and pride. Railroad-rate laws
reduced passenger fares and lowered the cost of shipping grain.

Kansas suffragettes in Lawrence in the early 1900s

Direct primaries were instituted to give people a greater voice in
the government, and Kansas women won the right to vote.
Workmen's compensation and child labor laws, stronger banking
regulations, and health reforms made life better for Kansans.

Advances in farming and technology also changed life in
Kansas. Steam- and gas-powered tractors and threshing machines
made plowing and harvesting easier. Crop yields increased as
farmers adopted improved "dry-farming" techniques. New crops
such as sorghum, sugar beets, broomcorn, and alfalfa sprouted in
abundance across the plains. Through fifty years of hardship,
Kansas had remained best known as "Bleeding Kansas." By the
1900s, however, the state's progressive attitude had changed that.
"Now it's leading Kansas and feeding Kansas, and everything but
needing Kansas," observed Philadelphia newspaperman Leigh
Mitchell Hodges.

WORLD WAR I AND THE ROARING TWENTIES

"Win the War with Wheat," blared the Topeka *Daily Capital*. World War I was raging in Europe, and as the United States joined in the fight, in April 1917, patriotic Kansans vowed to do their part. To feed the United States military and the starving people of war-torn Europe, Kansas farmers worked from dawn to dusk. Tractor plows turned up acres of previously untouched buffalo grass and many western counties doubled their production of wheat to meet the great demand. Some eighty thousand Kansans enlisted in the armed forces. Training facilities at Fort Leavenworth and at Camp Funston on the Fort Riley reservation molded recruits into fighting soldiers.

The final defeat of Germany in November 1918 brought the American troops marching home in triumph. In 1917, the Kansas legislature had passed a "bone dry" law outlawing completely the sale of liquor in the state. Other states demanded the adoption of the "Kansas idea," and in 1919, Americans passed the Eighteenth Amendment to the U.S. Constitution, under which national prohibition became law.

The 1920s brought excitement and change to Kansas in many ways. Increasingly, automobiles banged along country roads and laborers paved new, smoother highways. Kansan Walter Chrysler developed an important automobile company. Inventor Clyde Cessna, of Kingman County, thrilled spectators when he flew his airplanes across the Kansas skies.

In November 1919, angry coal miners in southeastern Kansas, demanding better working conditions, threw down their tools and formed picket lines. To halt the strike, Governor Henry Allen created a new state agency, the Court of Industrial Relations. Between 1920 and 1925, this unique three-man court ruled on many state labor disputes and attracted national attention. Newspaperman William Allen White argued repeatedly that the court interfered with strikers' freedom of speech. In the end, the United States Supreme Court agreed and overturned most of the labor court's decisions, calling them unconstitutional.

White conducted another important crusade in the 1920s against members of the Ku Klux Klan, who paraded the streets of Kansas hooded in white sheets. Anti-Jewish, anti-Catholic, and anti-black, the KKK preached hatred throughout the state. In response, White wrote boldly in his newspaper, "It is an organization of cowards. Not a man in it has the courage of his convictions. . . . The Ku Klux Klan in the community is a menace to peace and decent neighborly living." White promoted his campaign against the KKK by running for governor as an independent candidate in 1924. White lost the election, but in 1925, the state government refused to issue the KKK a charter, and in effect closed the organization down in Kansas.

THE DUST-BOWL YEARS

Kansans celebrated loudly when Senator Charles Curtis of Topeka was elected vice-president of the United States in 1928. Part Kaw Indian, Curtis was the only person of Indian ancestry ever to hold that office. His success in winning the vice-presidency, however, was the last good news many Kansans enjoyed for a long time.

The Wall Street stock market crash of October 1929 plunged the entire country into the worst depression in its history. During the next two years, Kansas crop prices dropped steadily. Then, in 1931, a long period of terrible drought began. Cruel heat ruined crops and turned the soil to dust. Winds blew up great dust

A Kansas farmstead during a dust storm in the 1930s

storms that choked the air and turned the Great Plains into a huge
"dust bowl." After one dust blizzard in 1935, the Garden City
Daily Telegram reported: "Bright electric signs could hardly be
seen across the street. Traffic was halted, schools closed." Blinded
by dust, people sometimes got lost in their own backyards. As
farms failed, thousands of families abandoned the state, while
other people wandered country roads and city streets in a
hopeless search for work.

In 1932, Kansans elected Republican Alfred M. Landon as
governor. Landon acted quickly to bring relief to Kansas farmers
and businessmen. Under his administration, the state legislature
reorganized state banks, cut taxes, and passed a law halting
mortgage foreclosures for a period of six months. Although
Americans repealed national prohibition in 1933, Landon backed
Kansas voters' demands that Kansas remain a "dry" state. In
Washington, new Democratic President Franklin D. Roosevelt

Kansas Governor Alf Landon, shown here kissing a baby while on the campaign trail, was the Republican presidential candidate in 1936.

worked hard to end the nation's economic woes. Landon welcomed many of Roosevelt's "New Deal" policies into Kansas. The federal Works Progress Administration (WPA) gave laborers jobs constructing libraries, schools, and post offices. At camps run by the Civilian Conservation Corps (CCC), young men dug lakes, built roads, and planted trees.

By 1936, hopeful Republicans believed Alf Landon might beat Roosevelt in that year's presidential election, and gave him their party's nomination. At rallies across the nation, Republican supporters shouted the slogan "Life, Liberty, and Landon." On their lapels, they wore Landon campaign buttons that featured bright yellow Kansas sunflowers. On election day, however, the hugely popular Roosevelt defeated Landon easily.

A number of military training bases operated in Kansas during World War II, including Fort Riley, a training center for the United States Cavalry.

WORLD WAR II AND PROSPERITY

Japanese warplanes swooped down in a surprise attack on the United States naval base at Pearl Harbor, Hawaii, on December 7, 1941. The next day, the United States declared war on the Axis nations of Japan, Germany, and Italy. Thousands of people throughout Kansas quickly volunteered to fight. More than 215,000 Kansans served in the military during World War II. Soldiers marched at old Camp Funston and Fort Leavenworth as well as at Camp Phillips, near Salina. Navy fliers soared into the air at training bases in Olathe and Hutchinson, while army air force pilots practiced at airfields in Garden City, Winfield, Pratt, Independence, Dodge City, and several other Kansas towns.

Kansas industry pitched into the war effort, as well. Plants in Wichita and Kansas City manufactured more than twenty-five thousand aircraft, including more than half of the nation's B-29 "Super Fortresses." Workers produced munitions materials at a Baxter Springs factory and at the Sunflower Ordnance Works near De Soto. Kansas women toiled at the artillery shell factory at Parsons. The war's demand for foodstuffs greatly revived the state's agricultural economy. Under sunny skies, farmers plowed their wheat fields and planted new acreage with such valuable crops as soybeans.

In August 1945, the war was brought to an end when American atomic bombs dropped on the Japanese cities of Hiroshima and Nagasaki. By that time, with a busy labor force and high crop prices, Kansans were enjoying a new level of prosperity. As America's victorious war veterans returned home, Kansans felt a special pride. General Dwight D. Eisenhower had grown up in Abilene. As supreme commander of the Allied forces in Europe, "Ike" Eisenhower had won international fame as one of the war's great heroes. When the highly decorated soldier returned to visit Kansas in June 1945, it was obvious that he had not forgotten his hometown roots. "The proudest thing I can say today," he declared simply, "is that I'm from Abilene."

THE EISENHOWER YEARS

Americans could not have been more surprised "if all the leopards in the nation's zoos had changed their spots overnight," exclaimed *American Magazine* reporter Clarence Woodbury in 1948. That year Kansas voters at last repealed prohibition in their state. Though many nondrinking citizens complained, some counties soon allowed the sale of hard alcohol in liquor stores.

In 1952, Abilene native Dwight D. Eisenhower (with arms outstretched) was elected president of the United States.

Change came to Kansas in other ways as well. In 1948, farmers organized the Kansas Association of Wheat Growers to develop more profitable farming methods. In July 1951, the Kansas River flooded suddenly, sending deep swirling waters through many central Kansas communities. To prevent costly floods elsewhere, engineers constructed important dams on the Smoky Hill River at Kanopolis, on the Fall River in Greenwood County, and on the Blue River north of Manhattan.

Republicans throughout Kansas cheered wildly during the presidential campaign of 1952. Their native son Dwight D. Eisenhower won the election by a wide margin. Eisenhower's successful eight years in the White House left Americans feeling good about the nation and themselves. President Eisenhower's brother, Milton, also made Kansans proud. A respected educator and president of Kansas State College, Milton Eisenhower headed the important United Nations Educational, Scientific and Cultural Organization (UNESCO) during its earliest days.

The growth of new manufacturing industries caused many Kansans to move from the countryside into the cities. New highways, such as the Kansas Turnpike, completed in 1956, made travel easier for many workers. In the early 1960s, as the population shifted, the state organized a new school-district system to meet changing needs. In 1954, Kansas had made national news when the United States Supreme Court heard the case of *Brown vs. Board of Education of Topeka*. The father of an eleven-year-old black girl named Linda Brown had sued the Topeka Board of Education for not allowing his daughter to attend an all-white school. In a landmark decision, the court ruled unanimously that it is unconstitutional for public schools to be segregated by race. This historic decision resulted in the gradual desegregation of public schools across the nation.

KANSAS TODAY AND TOMORROW

Dwight D. Eisenhower's heart and soul "grew out of the richness of the Kansas soil," Kansas Senator Robert Dole has claimed. The same can be said of Senator Dole himself. Since 1969, the Russell native has ably served his state in Washington, D.C. As one of the nation's foremost Republicans, Dole became Senate majority leader in 1985, and served as chairman of the powerful Finance Committee from 1981 to 1987.

Although Alf Landon died in 1987, at the amazing age of one hundred, his daughter, Nancy Landon Kassebaum, carries on the family's Republican political tradition. Elected to the United States Senate in 1978, Kassebaum was America's first woman senator elected in her own right.

Many Kansas farmers prospered during the 1960s and 1970s. Hybrid seeds, feeds, and improved fertilizers helped farm output to rise to new levels. Still, a recession in the 1980s hurt many farm families. In the face of changing technology, unsteady crop prices,

Since World War II, Kansas has been an important producer of aircraft and aircraft parts. Today, Wichita is the world's leading producer of light airplanes (left).

and unpredictable weather, the state's farm population continued to shrink.

Even through the 1980s, however, unemployment remained low in Kansas. In cities and towns throughout the state, factory whistles blow each day as people rush to work. Meat packing, mining, flour milling, and petroleum refining rate among the state's most productive industries, and more aircraft and aircraft parts are assembled in Kansas than anywhere else in the nation.

Amelia Earhart, born in Atchison, gained international fame as a daring pilot in the 1930s. In 1937, her plane mysteriously disappeared in the Pacific during an attempt to fly around the world. But her soaring spirit remains alive in Kansas. In 1972, Captain Ron Evans, of Topeka, commanded the pilot ship during *Apollo 17*'s mission to the moon. More recently, astronauts Colonel Joe Engle of Chapman and Salina native Dr. Steven Hawley have zoomed into orbit aboard NASA space shuttles. As space exploration reaches into the twenty-first century, one can bet Kansas will be involved. Since the days of the earliest pioneers, hardy Kansans have pushed themselves onward. It is not surprising, therefore, that the state's motto still inspires them: "Ad Astra per Aspera," "To the Stars through Difficulties."

Chapter 7

GOVERNMENT AND THE ECONOMY

GOVERNMENT AND THE ECONOMY

Progress in a state is achieved by the energy of its government and the health of its economy. In Kansas, elected officials, businessmen, and farmers all work side by side, striving for the state's continued growth and success.

GOVERNMENT

Kansas's most important legal document is its original 1859 Wyandotte Constitution. Though it has been amended more than seventy-five times, this body of laws still governs Kansas. Like the federal government, Kansas's government is divided into three branches. The legislative branch creates and repeals laws. The judicial branch, or court system, interprets the laws. The executive branch, or office of the governor, enforces the laws.

The Kansas State Capitol, in Topeka, houses the state legislature and many of the executive offices. The Kansas legislature consists of two separate chambers. The senate has 40 members elected to four-year terms, while the house of representatives consists of 125 members elected to two-year terms. These legislators represent the state's 105 counties and 627 incorporated cities and towns. When in session, they vote new bills into law, amend old laws, and appropriate money to be spent by the government.

Kansas governors are elected to four-year terms. As the highest executive in the state, the governor oversees the operation of state agencies, controls state spending, and is the state's chief law enforcement officer.

When vacancies occur in the seven-member Kansas Supreme Court, as well as in the seven-member Kansas Court of Appeals, the governor makes new appointments. Every six years, Kansas voters decide whether to keep these justices in office. Public votes also fill the judicial seats in the state's 31 district courts. From their high benches, the members of the judicial branch listen to court cases and rule on the proper meanings of the state's laws.

By law, Kansas must operate on a responsible cash basis. To raise money for state programs, the government collects taxes on income, inheritance, motor fuel, cigarettes, and tobacco. Cities, counties, and school districts obtain additional funds from property taxes.

EDUCATION

"We grow twenty thousand plants a year and keep a pedigree on each one," boasted geneticist Bikram Gill as he worked in a research laboratory at Kansas State University. "The William Allen White School of Journalism is among the best in the nation," commented alumnus Dan Reeder while giving a tour of the University of Kansas. Kansans have every right to be proud of their learning institutions. The state has come a long way since the days of the first simple missionary schools for the Indians. Every year, Kansas taxpayers spend approximately $1.5 billion to educate the 282,000 elementary and 124,000 secondary school students that attend its public schools.

Many high school graduates continue their educations at the dozens of vocational schools, technical schools, colleges, and universities found in the state. With nearly twenty-seven

Left: The Hiawatha Theatre at Haskell Indian
Junior College
Above: The University of Kansas in Lawrence

thousand students, the University of Kansas at Lawrence is
Kansas's largest state-supported university. The university also
has campuses in Wichita and Kansas City. Other state-run schools
include Kansas State University at Manhattan, Wichita State
University, Emporia State University, Fort Hays State University,
and Pittsburg State University.

Baker University at Baldwin City, founded during the territorial
era, is the oldest of Kansas's private schools of higher learning.
Other outstanding private institutions include Benedictine College
at Atchison, Bethany College at Lindsborg, Bethel College at North
Newton, Marymount College at Salina, Ottawa University at
Ottawa, and Washburn University of Topeka. The Haskell Indian
Junior College, in Lawrence, was founded in 1884 to provide
educational opportunities for Native Americans.

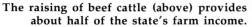
The raising of beef cattle (above) provides
about half of the state's farm income.

AGRICULTURE

The Wheat State and Breadbasket of the Nation are two of
Kansas's nicknames. In 1874, Mennonites from Russia came to
Kansas with sacks of a hardy wheat seed called "Turkey Red."
Since that time, Kansas has grown into the number-one wheat-
producing state, providing as much as 18 percent of the nation's
annual production. Only seven countries in the world harvest
more wheat each year than Kansas.

Grain sorghum (used as livestock feed), corn, soybeans, sugar
beets, oats, alfalfa, rye, and barley rank high among Kansas crops.
For years, orchards in northeastern Kansas and in Reno County
have yielded prizewinning apples.

Livestock represents a large portion of Kansas's agricultural
output. The state ranks second only to Texas in production of beef
cattle. In addition, dairy cows graze on Kansas pasturelands, and
farmers raise sheep, hogs, and poultry in rising numbers.

Kansas, the nation's leading producer of wheat (above), is also a major corn producer (left).

In the winter of 1989, freezing cold, drought, and high winds hurt farmers. "The wheat is already lost," mourned Salina farmer Darwin McCall. "All we can do now is try to save the land." Increased irrigation, new soil conservation methods, and improved dry-farming techniques have helped farmers through the years. The whims of the weather, however, will always make farming a challenge. In spite of that, on more than seventy-two thousand farms, Kansas's farmers still succeed.

MANUFACTURING AND SERVICE INDUSTRIES

More than 210,000 Kansans are involved in manufacturing. Milling and meat packing have always been two important Kansas industries. Currently, Kansas mills more flour than any other state, and the Iowa Beef Company's meat-packing plant outside Garden City is the largest in the world.

Kansas easily remains the nation's leader in aircraft production.

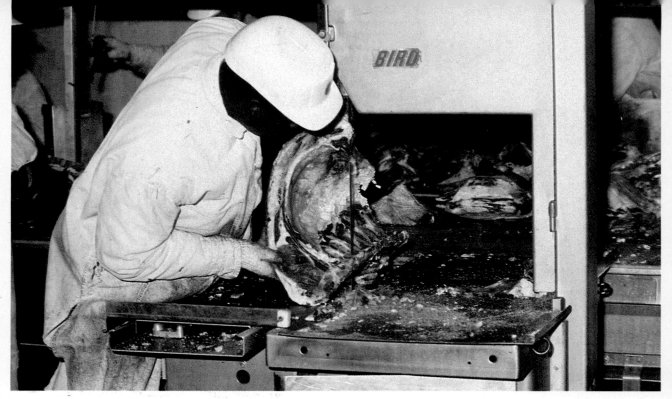

Meat packing is one of the state's leading industries.

With the Beech, Boeing, Cessna, and Learjet companies all centered in Wichita, that city rightfully claims the title "Air Capital of the world." Wichita is also the home of the Coleman Company, a leading manufacturer of insulated coolers and camping equipment. Goodyear tires are produced at a plant in Topeka, and automobiles roll off the assembly line at the General Motors plant in Kansas City. Other important industries in the state include the manufacture of farm equipment, clothing, chemicals, printed materials, and plastic products.

Kansas's large service economy helps keep the state's unemployment rate among the lowest in the nation. Kansas banks, real estate firms, and insurance companies offer a wide variety of services, and thousands of retail stores meet the daily needs of Kansas consumers. The H & R Block accounting firm, which has some eight thousand tax preparation outlets in fourteen countries, was founded in Kansas City over forty years ago by Henry and Richard Block. "Clean and Fast and Cheap" was the slogan of the first White Castle hamburger stand in Wichita in 1921. Today, that fast-food chain stretches across the nation. Even larger is the Pizza Hut restaurant chain, which began as a single restaurant in Wichita in 1958 and now boasts more than forty-five hundred locations nationwide.

NATURAL RESOURCES

Unusual limestone fence posts can be seen mile after mile along the edges of roads and fields in western Kansas. Because they lacked trees for wooden fence posts, inventive farmers long ago quarried post rock limestone and sawed it into suitable lengths. They then stretched wire from post to post to create fences that endure today.

Kansans have long valued the natural resources found beneath their soil. Today, quarried limestone deposits are crushed and used in the production of cement. Kansas gypsum, sand, clay, and gravel are also used extensively in the construction industries. Mining operations centered around Crawford and Cherokee counties have long produced large supplies of coal. Lead and zinc are two other valuable minerals mined in southeastern Kansas.

In 1892, drillers discovered oil at a well in Neodesha. That success led to other rich oil strikes throughout the state. The Hugoton Gas Field, one of the world's largest natural gas fields, extends beneath eight southwestern Kansas counties. So much helium is recovered annually in Rush, Pawnee, and Barton counties that Kansas leads the nation in the production of that gas.

Geologists claim that enough salt lies beneath the ground in Kansas to supply America's needs for half a million years. When salt mines near Hutchinson were emptied, businessmen found an additional use for them. The stable climate found deep within the ground provides perfect conditions for storing the films, records, and files of dozens of companies. Vaults in otherwise unused limestone caves near Kansas City serve the same valuable purpose.

TRANSPORTATION AND COMMUNICATION

The central location of Kansas makes it an important link in the nation's transportation system. Ranked fifth among the states in railroad mileage, the state has about 7,000 miles (11,265 kilometers) of track in active use. Freight service is provided by fourteen railroads. While the golden era of such passenger trains as the *Rocky Mountain Rocket, El Capitan,* and *Super Chief* is gone, passenger trains still stop in about a dozen Kansas cities.

Trucks and automobiles crisscross the state along a road network that covers more than 132,000 miles (212,428 kilometers). Interstate 70 is a major east-west route. Vehicles traveling north and south between Salina and Wichita use Interstate 135, while Interstate 35 is the busiest highway between Topeka and Wichita. In 1983, to honor the state's role in the film *The Wizard of Oz*, the Kansas legislature gave U.S. Highway 54 a special designation. Now motorists in southwestern Kansas may speed along the "Yellow Brick Road." With some 370 municipal and private airports dotting the landscape, air travel is also practical for many Kansans. In addition, six commercial airlines serve twelve Kansas cities.

The Carbondale *Astonisher and Paralyzer,* the Perry *Champion Liar,* and the Topeka *Saturday Night Wheeze* are just a few of the many newspapers once published in Kansas. Kansans have

The state's rich land yields a number of mineral resources, including coal (right), and limestone, used by early Kansas farmers to make fence posts (left).

always been eager to communicate information and ideas. Between 1835 and 1916, a total of 4,368 different newspapers were published in Kansas, more than in any other state. Today, some 250 newspapers are printed regularly, including about 50 dailies. The *Wichita Eagle-Beacon* has the largest circulation. Other important Kansas newspapers include the *Capital-Journal* of Topeka, the *Hutchinson News,* and the *Salina Journal.*

Kansas first tuned in to hear local radio when KFH in Wichita began broadcasting in 1922. About 125 Kansas radio stations currently provide listeners with music, news, and entertaining talk shows. Kansas television broadcasting started in the studios of KTVH in Hutchinson in 1953. Today, Kansans are served by about twenty television stations.

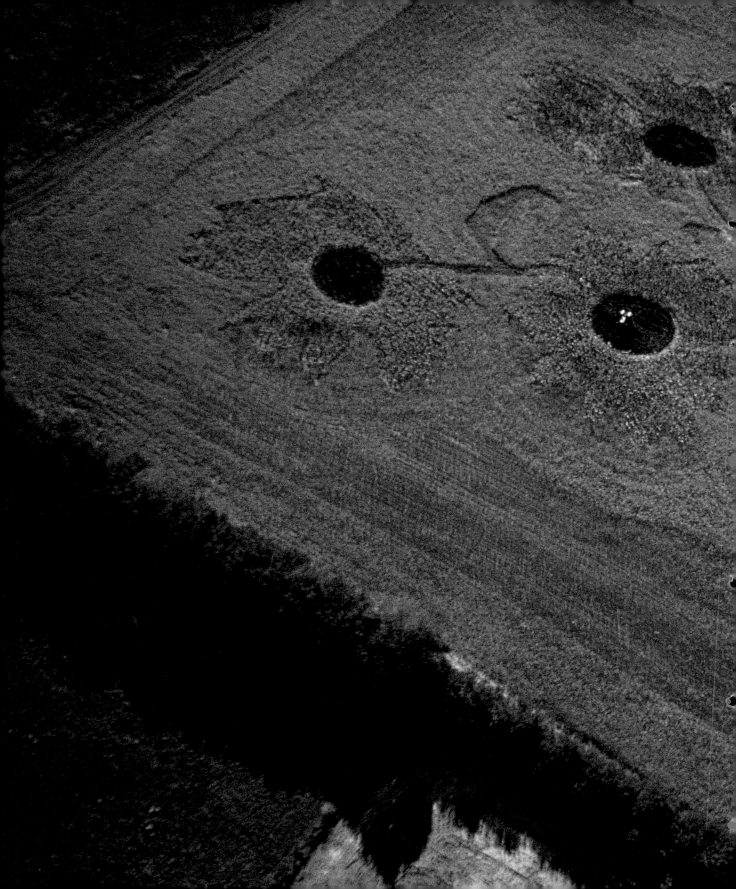

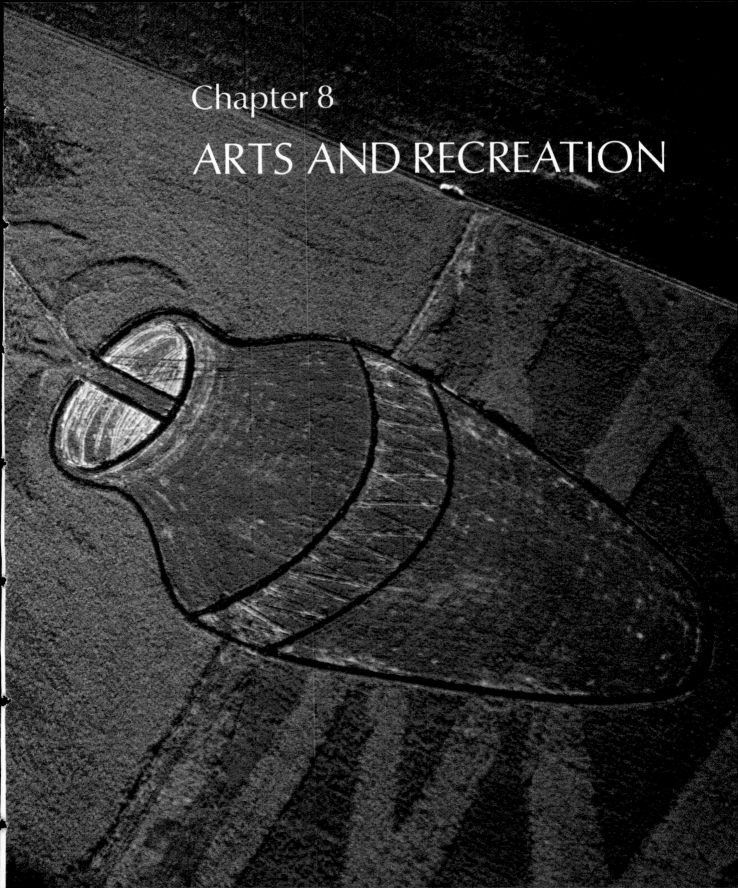

Chapter 8
ARTS AND RECREATION

ARTS AND RECREATION

FOLK CULTURE

Kansans preserve their special heritages by passing down ethnic traditions, tall tales, and local legends from generation to generation. The state's Mexican population celebrates its ethnic holidays with annual festivals in Topeka, Garden City, and other cities. Kansans of Bohemian heritage still call Thanksgiving *Cesky Dan* and gather at their holiday dinner tables to eat *kolacky* and *strudel*. Swedish Kansans travel each year to Lindsborg to enjoy the food, music, and dancing at the traditional Svensk Hyllningsfest held there. At Christmastime, German Kansans look forward to munching on little cookies called *pfeffernusse*.

Religious services, spelling bees, public book readings, picnics, and parties all gave Kansas pioneers opportunities to socialize. Today, harvest dances such as the Neewollah festival (Halloween spelled backwards), in Independence, still bring Kansans together.

For many years, tall tales have given Kansans a sense of pride and a way to laugh at adversity. Growing conditions are one thing about which Kansans like to brag. A story in the Coolidge *Border Ruffian* once boasted, "Stranger, you'll never know what a corn country is until you go to Kansas. . . . When the men are husking they carry along stepladders, which they place near the cornstalk. Two men then climb up and cut off the ears with a crosscut saw, letting them fall to the ground. Four horses are then hitched to each ear, and it is dragged to the crib." During the difficult times of the 1930s, farmers often joked grimly about the dust storms.

One story described dust so thick that a prairie dog was seen digging a burrow ten feet in the air. Another claimed that birds were flying backwards to keep the dust out of their eyes.

Old Indian legends have been a part of Kansas history as well. One tale tells of two Indian lovers who drowned in a river while trying to elope. Soon they returned to the water's surface in the form of graceful swans. When French explorers heard this legend, they named the river the *Marais des Cygnes,* the "Marsh of the Swans." Another legend described how the famous Waconda Springs, once found in Mitchell County, got its name. A brokenhearted Indian maiden named Waconda threw herself into the waters after the warrior she loved was killed.

The most famous legend passed down to Kansans is that of the mythical Jayhawk. A popular version tells of an Irishman named Pat Devlin, who lived in Kansas during the territorial wars of 1856. Devlin was returning home after a day of plundering across the border in Missouri, when someone pointed at Devlin's stolen goods and asked what he had been doing. "You know in Ireland," Devlin supposedly replied, "we have a bird called the Jayhawk, which makes its living off other birds. I guess you might say I have been Jayhawking." Kansas's free-staters were soon referred to as "Jayhawkers." In truth, there is no such bird as the Jayhawk—supposedly a cross between the mischievous blue jay and soaring hawk. But Kansans have grown to identify with the independent, fighting spirit of this mythical bird, and proudly call themselves "Jayhawkers" and their state the "Jayhawker State."

MUSIC AND ART

Some of Kansas's most valuable cultural contributions are its folk songs. Americans everywhere know "Home on the Range,"

John Steuart Curry, shown here painting a mural for the United States Department of Justice building, gained nationwide fame for his simple, straightforward scenes of American rural life.

the official song of Kansas. This 1873 song, written by Smith County neighbors Dr. Brewster Higley and Dan Kelley, describes an ideal land where deer and antelope roam beneath cloudless skies.

Along cattle trails and on pioneer homesteads, Kansas cowboys and settlers made up songs to fill idle hours. "Comin' Back to Kansas," "The Kansas Jayhawker Song," and "The Dewey-Berry Song" are all examples of uniquely Kansas tunes. The song "Kansas Land" contains the following cheerful chorus:

Oh Kansas girls, sweet Kansas girls,
With sky-blue eyes and flaxen curls—
They sing and dance and flirt and play
And when a boyfriend comes that way
They meet him at the sod house door,
Then be with him forever more.

Popular local brass bands, with drums booming and cornets tooting, marched along the streets of many Kansas towns in the 1880s. Since 1882, people have journeyed to Lindsborg to hear Handel's *Messiah* sung at the Easter festival held there. Other towns, such as Emporia and Newton, also present yearly performances of classical religious music. Opera houses and music halls throughout the state give Kansans a chance to listen to the best of the world's musical composers.

Some talented pioneers carried sketchbooks and oil paints with them to Kansas. The portraits, landscapes, and illustrations painted in the late 1800s by such men as Henry Worrall and Samuel J. Reader initiated Kansas's rich artistic tradition. In the early 1900s, Topekan George M. Stone and Bethany College professor Sven Birger Sandzen both earned reputations as innovative painters. Visitors to the state capitol grounds in Topeka admire *Pioneer Woman of Kansas*, a sculpture by Robert Merrell Gage that was dedicated in 1937.

In the 1930s, John Steuart Curry—by far the state's most famous artist—painted striking murals in the state capitol depicting Kansas history. Other Curry paintings, such as *Baptism in Kansas*, *Tornado Over Kansas*, and *Kansas Wheat Ranch*, established him as an artist of national importance.

One must be in a plane to really appreciate the art of Stanley J. Herd. In 1981, this Kansas-born muralist began using wheat fields as canvases for spectacular artworks. He creates this "crop art" by using plows and disks to carve the land. "Each implement turns the ground another way, and I [use] them like different pencils," he has explained. His 1988 project, done for a celebration at Haskell Indian Junior College in Lawrence, was a stunning, 1,000-foot- (305-meter-) long portrait of a Native American.

LITERATURE

"All's set!" is finally heard from some teamster. . . . "All's set," is directly responded from every quarter. "Stretch out!" immediately [yells] the captain. Then, "heps!" of drivers—the cracking of whips—the trampling of feet—the occasional creak of wheels—the rumbling of wagons—form a new scene of exquisite confusion, which I shall not attempt further to describe. "Fall in!" is heard from headquarters, and the wagons are forthwith strung out upon the long inclined plain, which stretches to the heights beyond Council Grove.

In his 1844 book *Commerce of the Prairies*, Josiah Gregg described vividly the history of the Santa Fe Trail. Since the earliest days of Spanish exploration, people have been writing about Kansas. *Six Months in Kansas*, by Mrs. Hannah H. Ropes; and *Kansas: Its Interior and Exterior Life*, by Sara T. L. Robinson, were both popular 1856 books that revealed pioneer life in the territory. Mark Twain used Kansas Senator Samuel Pomeroy's political scandal as the centerpiece of his 1873 novel *The Gilded Age*, written with Charles D. Warner. Atchison journalist E. W. Howe, called the "Sage of Potato Hill," helped launch the American Realism movement in literature with his stark 1883 novel *The Story of a Country Town*. Fort Scott newspaperman Eugene Fitch Ware published poetry under the pen name Ironquill, including the popular 1908 book *The Rhymes of Ironquill*.

In the 1930s, Laura Ingalls Wilder wrote a series of children's books based on her life growing up in the Midwest. The third book of the series, *Little House on the Prairie*, described the years she and her family spent in a log cabin on the Kansas prairie.

The best known of Kansas's native writers is William Allen White. White's autobiography, published after his death, won a Pulitzer Prize in 1946. White's son, William L. White, succeeded

Left: An illustration from Laura Ingalls Wilder's *Little House on the Prairie*, which described the years she spent as a child in Kansas
Above: Noted Kansas writer and editor William Allen White

his father as editor of the Emporia *Gazette*. His nonfiction book *They Were Expendable*, published in 1942, described the dangerous exploits of a World War II PT boat squadron.

William Inge, who was born in Independence, won fame as a playwright in the 1950s. Such dramas as *Come Back Little Sheba*, *Bus Stop*, *The Dark at the Top of the Stairs*, and *Picnic*, for which he won a Pultizer Prize, examined the daily lives and social problems of people in small midwestern towns.

"The village of Holcomb stands on the high wheat plains of western Kansas," wrote writer Truman Capote, "a lonesome area that other Kansans call 'out there.'" In 1959, Capote journeyed to Holcomb to investigate the tragic murders of the Clutter family. Capote's 1966 book *In Cold Blood*, a novelistic account of the story, has been called the greatest American "nonfiction novel."

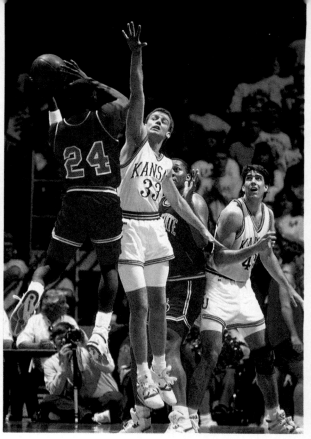

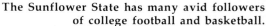
The Sunflower State has many avid followers
of college football and basketball.

SPORTS AND OUTDOOR RECREATION

From time to time, the excitement of Kansas sports fans spreads
across the state like a prairie fire. Basketball fans always seem to
have plenty to cheer about. For decades, the University of Kansas
Jayhawks, members of the Big Eight Conference, have ranked
among the best in college basketball. The skills of center Wilt
Chamberlain—who went on to become a legendary professional
star—dazzled Jayhawk fans in the early 1960s. Kansans honked
horns and danced in the streets when the Jayhawks won the 1988
national title in the NCAA tournament. The Wildcats of Kansas
State University and the Wheat Shockers of Wichita State also
regularly field top contending basketball teams. The Fort Hays
State Tigers won back-to-back national championships in the
NAIA basketball tournament in 1984 and 1985.

Lovers of professional sports follow the Kansas City Royals baseball team and the Kansas City Chiefs football team on television, or travel over the border to Missouri to see the games in person. Many baseball greats grew up in Kansas. Hall of Famer Walter "Big Train" Johnson of Humboldt pitched a record 416 professional victories before he retired in 1927. Muscotah's Joe Tinker expertly relayed baseballs while a shortstop on the Chicago Cubs. His part in the famed infield combination of "Tinker to Evers to Chance" won him a place in the Baseball Hall of Fame in 1946.

As a football running back at the University of Kansas, Gale Sayers earned the nickname "The Kansas Comet." Sayers went on to break a number of professional records while playing for the Chicago Bears. Centralia's John Riggins broke records as a running back for the New York Jets and the Washington Redskins. Jayhawkers were delighted when Riggins was named the Super Bowl's Most Valuable Player in 1982.

Early Kansas settlers enjoyed competing in foot races. Since that time, running has remained an important tradition in the state. Elkhart's Glenn Cunningham set world records in the mile and 1,500-meter runs in 1936. Jim Ryun of Wichita won headlines by setting world records in the mile, half-mile, and 1,500-meter runs in the 1960s.

"The Vermillion contains some fine large fish and many a large cat-fish filled our hungry maws," wrote an 1850s traveler on the Oregon Trail. For years, fishermen hooked record-sized catfish of 100 pounds (45 kilograms) and more on such rivers as the Vermillion, Republican, and Kansas. Catfish, bass, bluegill, and walleye are among the plentiful fish that can be caught along Kansas streams and lakes. In summertime, forty state lakes welcome energetic campers, swimmers, water-skiers, and boaters.

Chapter 9
HIGHLIGHTS OF KANSAS

HIGHLIGHTS OF KANSAS

"If I went west, I think I would go to Kansas," Abraham
Lincoln once remarked. Through the years, the allure of Kansas
has affected many Americans. Today, a traveler crisscrossing the
state might want to see some of the following attractions.

NORTHEASTERN KANSAS

Every day, thousands of commuters pour across the Missouri
border to jobs in Kansas City, Kansas. Kansas City citizens
welcome tourists to their metropolitan region, too. History buffs
enjoy visiting the 1856 Grinter House, site of the first Kansas
River ferry crossing. The American farmer is honored in nearby
Bonner Springs at the Agricultural Hall of Fame, which houses
America's largest and most varied collection of agricultural
artifacts. Every fall, Bonner Springs hosts the Renaissance Festival,
one of the state's most popular events.

The Kansas City suburb of Mission Hills, with its stately
mansions and manicured lawns, is one of the loveliest
neighborhoods in the nation. Visitors to nearby Fairway may
walk the grounds of the Shawnee Methodist Mission. Founded in
1830, this Indian school marked a starting point of the Santa Fe
and Oregon trails.

"Four tents, all on one street, a barrel of water or whiskey
under a tree, and a pot on a pole over the fire." That is how a

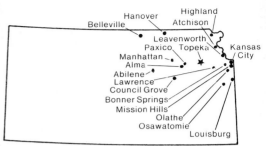

Bonner Springs is the home of the Agricultural Hall of Fame, which houses the nation's largest collection of agricultural artifacts.

traveler described Leavenworth in 1854. The city has changed considerably since then. Fort Leavenworth, however, has remained in constant use since its establishment in 1827. Army officers, when asked, politely direct tourists to the Post Museum, which holds the nation's largest collection of horse-drawn vehicles.

To the north is Atchison, where tourists may visit the birthplace of famed pilot Amelia Earhart. The Atchison County Museum also contains interesting Earhart items. Those interested in Doniphan County history travel to Highland and visit the Highland Presbyterian Mission. Built in 1837, this mission to the Iowa, Fox, and Sac Indians was the county's first white settlement.

A stop in Olathe is a must for tourists driving south of Kansas City. The Mahaffie Farmstead preserves a stop along the Santa Fe Trail. Olathe's Prairie Center offers miles of trails where hikers can learn the natural history of Kansas's tall-grass prairie. Farther south, at the Louisburg Cider Mill, visitors can watch the pressing of apples and afterward enjoy cups of fresh, sweet cider. The name

John Brown still looms large in the town of Osawatomie. The John Brown Museum is located there in an old log cabin once used by the fiery abolitionist.

University of Kansas students carry their books along the streets of historic downtown Lawrence. Many KU graduates are featured in the city's Kansas All-Sports Hall of Fame. Tourists also marvel at the fossils exhibited at KU's Dyche Museum of Natural History.

Topeka, the state's capital, has a number of special attractions. The Topeka Zoo features wild birds in a tropical rain forest and the thrill of a walk-through gorilla cage. The dome of the Kansas State Capitol rises high above most Topeka buildings. A walk inside the capitol is highlighted by John Steuart Curry's famous murals. Another important Topeka landmark is the Menninger Foundation. Established in 1925 by Dr. C. F. Menninger and his sons Dr. Karl and Dr. William Menninger, it is considered one of the world's leading mental-health centers.

Farm machinery from the late 1800s draws tourists to the Wabaunsee County Historical Museum in Alma. Perhaps even more interesting is the Flint Hills Scenic Tour, offered in Paxico. Among the engaging sites along the tour are a pheasant farm, a one-hundred-head herd of buffalo, and miles of beautiful tall-grass prairie. To the southwest, in Council Grove, is the 1857 Last Chance Store, which was the last supply stop on the Santa Fe Trail. The old Kaw Methodist Mission, also in Council Grove, reminds Kansans of their pioneer heritage.

Kansas State University provides residents of Manhattan with cultural events and sports activities. Manhattanites like to call their city the "Little Apple" as opposed to the "Big Apple" of New York City's Manhattan. Farther north, in Hanover, is the Hollenberg Pony Express Station. Built in 1857, it is the only original and unaltered such station left standing in the nation.

The Dwight D. Eisenhower Library at the Eisenhower Center in Abilene

The solemn remains of an ancient Pawnee Indian village are visible near Belleville. Fort Riley near Junction City, once the home of Indian-fighter General George Custer, is still a busy military base. The excitement of the Wild West can be felt at Old Abilene Town in Abilene. Abilene's Eisenhower Center contains a wealth of information about President Dwight D. Eisenhower. After touring the president's boyhood home, visitors can pay their respects at his burial site.

SOUTHEASTERN KANSAS

Both the enchanting beauty of the land and the wonder of its history continually lure tourists to southeastern Kansas. In Linn County near Pleasanton, visitors to the Marais des Cygnes and Trading Post museums can view guns, farm tools, and other fascinating items from the state's "Bleeding Kansas" period.

Twenty buildings, including a hospital, officers' quarters, and guardhouse still stand at Fort Scott in neighboring Bourbon County. Strolling through the 1842 military post, visitors learn about life during Kansas's frontier days.

The state's mining heritage draws tourists to Columbus, where the astonishing sixteen-story-high coal shovel "Big Brutus" houses a miners' museum. Kansas miners once opened great "strip pits" near Oswego. In recent years, however, more than 8,000 acres (3,238 hectares) of the scarred land have been reclaimed as a wildlife area. The same is true in Parsons, where anglers and hunters find fish and game at the Mined-land Wildlife Area.

"So there she stands—this Kansas of ours, a robust hard-working wholesome old girl," wrote William Allen White proudly in an issue of the world-famous Emporia *Gazette*. Travelers through Emporia can buy the latest copy of the newspaper, now edited by White's granddaughter. Farther west, Fred Harvey's Harvey House restaurant and hotel still stands in Florence. It is now a museum that describes the interesting history of the "Harvey Girls," who dressed in prim black and white uniforms and served guests with good manners and efficiency.

Mennonite emigrants helped settle Marion County, and their story is told at the Mennonite Heritage Museum in Goessel. In nearby Hillsboro, the state's cultural heritage comes alive in an annual spring folk festival full of music and ethnic foods. At the Maxwell Game Preserve north of Canton, the quiet grandeur of nature reigns as buffalo and elk roam free on 4,000 acres (1,619 hectares) of fenced prairie.

Tourists can get a taste of pioneer life on a Flint Hills Overland Wagon trip. The trip, which begins in El Dorado, is made in covered wagons and coaches and includes campfire meals on the

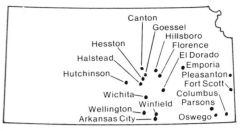

Visitors to southeastern Kansas can take a Flint Hills Overland Wagon trip (left) or explore historic Fort Scott (above).

prairie. Travelers who like to pick their own vegetables will enjoy a visit to the Spring Hill Farm in Winfield. Banjo pickers and fiddlers from all over the nation gather in Winfield each September to entertain crowds with music and fun at the Walnut Valley Bluegrass Festival.

During the 1893 Oklahoma land rush, more than a hundred thousand excited settlers poured into the Cherokee Strip in a single day. At the Cherokee Strip Land Rush Museum in Arkansas City, visitors learn about the history of that thrilling border region. In the 1870s, cowboys regularly drove cattle through Sumner County. The Chisholm Trail Museum in Wellington captures the spirit of the cattle drives and tells about the lifestyle of Kansas settlers.

Of course, many of the great cattle drives ended at the Wichita stockyards. "Leave your revolvers at police headquarters. . . .

Wichita is the largest city in Kansas.

Carrying concealed weapons strictly forbidden," a sign outside
Wichita once warned rowdy cowboys. Today, the Old Cowtown
Museum re-creates the lively Wichita of the 1870s with thirty
authentic buildings, including a jail, blacksmith shop, and general
store.

Bustling Wichita is filled with other fascinating museums as
well. The Wichita Sedgwick County Historical Museum features
vivid exhibits on the history of early Wichita and Sedgwick
County, including a replica of a 1910 drugstore. The Children's
Museum allows young visitors to interact with colorful science,
health, and communications exhibits. Many masterpieces of
American art are displayed at the Wichita Art Museum. Wichita
State University also offers visitors a fine art museum, as well as a
museum of anthropology. Native American culture is preserved at
the Mid-America All-Indian Center and Museum.

At the Wheat Bin in Hesston, visitors watch wheat milled into flour the old-fashioned way. The fresh breads and buns that are sold at the Wheat Bin bakery smell and taste delicious. A few miles south, in Halstead, is the Kansas Health Museum, which features exhibits on health care and how the human body functions.

A "moon buggy," original spacecraft, and spacesuits amaze visitors at the Kansas Cosmophere and Space Center in Hutchinson. The center features a space camp and a thrilling planetarium. Thousands of people crowd into Hutchinson every September to take part in the Kansas State Fair. Livestock shows, carousel rides, and stock-car races make the fair a huge event.

NORTHWESTERN KANSAS

The high plains beckon travelers heading into northwestern Kansas. Just outside Minneapolis is Rocky City, where centuries of underground water activity have shaped sandstone into perfect spheres and ellipses. Parents enjoy picnic lunches there while their children play hide-and-seek among the unusual large rocks. The remains of a Pawnee earth lodge that is nearly two hundred years old are the centerpiece of the Pawnee Indian Village Museum in Republic County. Artifacts excavated there reveal how the Pawnees lived in the early 1800s.

Wilson, called the "Czech Capital of Kansas," hosts an After Harvest Czech Festival every July. Participants dance lively polkas and munch on tasty kolacky and other native Czech foods. Farther north, in Lucas, cars drive slowly past the strange home of S. P. Dinsmoor. In 1907, Dinsmoor began sculpting limestone, wood, and cement to create the jungle on his lawn that he called his "Garden of Eden." Curiosity about the history of oil drilling

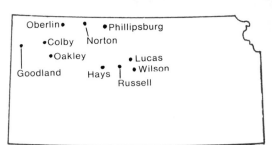

Northwestern Kansas features such stunning rock formations as Castle Rock (right) and Monument Rocks (above).

brings tourists to Russell's Oil Patch Museum, which features a collection of oil-field artifacts and equipment.

Every summer, Phillipsburg hosts a huge rodeo where crowds cheer loudly as they watch such exciting competitions as bronco breaking and steer roping. The nearby town of Norton, often called the "Pheasant Capital of the World," is a mecca for game-bird hunters. History buffs find the replica of Norton's old Stage Station 15 worth visiting.

The city of Hays offers visitors a self-guided tour through streets once roamed by such legendary figures as Wild Bill Hickok and Buffalo Bill. In addition, the restored buildings at historic Fort Hays re-create everyday life at an 1860s frontier outpost.

Decatur County homesteaders suffered terribly at the hands of

Dull Knife and his North Cheyenne warriors in 1878. Exhibits at the Decatur County Museum in Oberlin give details of that last bloody Indian raid on Kansas soil. Displays in the High Plains Museum in Goodland show how Kansas pioneers survived on the prairies. The Thomas County Historical Museum in Colby has such a valuable collection of antique artifacts that it is sometimes referred to as the "Little Smithsonian."

Tourists notice jutting Castle Rock long before they reach the 70-foot- (21-meter-) high chalk spire in Grove County. This eerie natural landmark has been shaped by centuries of whistling winds. Farther west along the Smoky Hill River, at Monument Rocks National Landmark, are a number of other tall chalk bluffs and natural pyramids. Through the years, archaeologists have discovered many fabulous fossils in the chalky cliffs there. Many are on display at the Fick Fossil and History Museum in Oakley. Oakley's Prairie Dog Town features live animals native to Kansas. Visitors are permitted to feed the tame deer, goats, foxes, prairie dogs, and other animals at this popular petting zoo.

SOUTHWESTERN KANSAS

"All sorts of water birds swarmed around from all sides. Never have I seen such quantities of swans, cranes, pelicans, geese, and ducks as were here," marveled Dr. Frederick Wislizenus during an 1841 visit to Cheyenne Bottoms. Located north of Great Bend, this 41,000-acre (16,592-hectare) marshland still provides habitats for hundreds of thousands of migrating birds. Southeast of Great Bend, the Quivira National Wildlife Refuge is also a bird-watcher's paradise. Such fascinating birds as bald eagles and peregrine falcons swoop among the refuge's sand dunes and cottonwood trees.

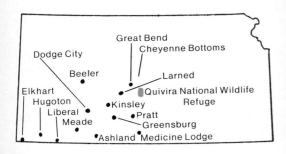

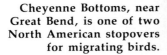

Cheyenne Bottoms, near Great Bend, is one of two North American stopovers for migrating birds.

The busy days of the Santa Fe Trail seem to come alive on the road between Great Bend and Larned. The natural landmark of Pawnee Rock served as an Indian lookout and ambush spot along the dusty route. Fort Larned was established in 1859 to protect travelers on the trail. Visitors to Fort Larned National Historic Site may tour restored fort buildings and examine original wagon ruts leading south to Santa Fe.

One of the world's largest freshwater fish hatcheries operates in Pratt. The Kansas Fish and Game Museum in Pratt invites visitors to learn about the hatchery process and visit a freshwater aquarium.

Two curiosities cause people to stop their cars in Greensburg. The town boasts both the world's largest hand-dug well, and the world's largest Pallasite meteorite. The well, dug in 1887, served the town for fifty years. Scientists have determined that the 1,000-pound (454-kilogram) meteorite, which was found near Greensburg in 1949, plunged to earth some two thousand years ago. Several miles to the north, Kinsley offers cross-country

Dodge City features a replica of Front Street as it looked in the 1870s.

travelers an ideal rest stop. Signs in that town boast that it is the exact halfway point between San Francisco and New York City.

In traditional dress, hundreds of proud Native Americans gather in Medicine Lodge every three years. There, the signing of the historic 1867 Indian Peace Treaty is reenacted amid the colorful pageantry of native dances and music.

Memories of the Wild West are awakened at Dodge City. Gunfighting actors in search of action stalk along Historic Front Street past the swinging doors of the Long Branch Saloon. The ghosts of real cowboys and horse thieves seem to haunt Dodge City's old Boot Hill Cemetery.

The Pioneer Museum in Ashland offers visitors a chance to study the less violent lifestyles of Kansas's hardworking homesteaders, while a museum outside Beeler honors the memory

Every year, Liberal hosts an International Pancake Derby.

of famed scientist George Washington Carver, who once lived in
Ness County.

One hundred years ago, the Dalton Gang used the Meade home
of their sister, Eva Dalton Whipple, as a hideout. Visitors can pass
through the secret tunnel that the bank robbers constructed
between the farmhouse and the barn for speedy escapes. An even
more famous home is Dorothy's House in Liberal, an exact replica
of Dorothy Gale's house in the 1939 film *The Wizard of Oz*.
Dorothy's house was supposedly launched skyward by a
tornado—but more conventional aircraft can be seen at the Liberal
Air Museum, which celebrates the heritage of American aviation.

Every year since 1950, fun-loving Liberal citizens have run an
International Pancake Derby on Shrove Tuesday. The event, held
in competition with women from Olney, England, consists of
housewives running a course while flipping pancakes in their
skillets.

The Peace Treaty Pageant at Medicine Lodge

For decades, natural gas deposits have brought prosperity to Stevens County. The story of gas exploration in the region is told at the Gas and Historical Museum in Hugoton. Not far away, buffalo and other prairie animals roam across the plains of the Finney County Wildlife Area. Elkhart also offers travelers a look at the glory of the Jayhawker State. On the high plains of the Cimarron National Grasslands, Kansas retains the same natural beauty first discovered by Coronado in 1541.

From corner to corner, Kansas fills visitors with fascination. Friendly people and vivid sights await all who venture into America's heartland. Traveling poet Vachel Lindsay may have summed up the feeling best when he wrote in 1912, "I have crossed the mystic border. I have left Earth. I have entered Wonderland. . . . This morning I passed the stone mile-post that marks the beginning of Kansas."

KANSAS

FACTS AT A GLANCE

GENERAL INFORMATION

Statehood: January 29, 1861, thirty-fourth state

Origin of Name: named after the Indians that the Sioux called the Kansa, meaning "people of the south wind"

State Capital: Topeka, capital since 1861

State Nicknames: Sunflower State, Wheat State, Jayhawker State, and Midway, U.S.A.

State Flag: The Kansas flag consists of a dark blue field with the state seal in the center. A sunflower on a bar of twisted gold lies above the seal, and below the seal is the word "Kansas." The seal contains a landscape that includes a rising sun, representing the east; and a river and steamboat, representing commerce. In the foreground, a settler's cabin and a man plowing a field represent agriculture. A wagon train heads west, and buffalo are seen fleeing from two Indians. Around the top of the seal is a cluster of thirty-four stars. The state motto appears above the stars.

State Motto: *Ad Astra per Aspera*, Latin words meaning "To the Stars through Difficulties"

State Flower: Sunflower

State Bird: Western meadowlark

State Tree: Cottonwood

State Animal: Buffalo

State Song: "Home on the Range," lyrics by Brewster Higley, music by Daniel Kelley:

> Oh, give me a home where the buffalo roam,
> Where the deer and the antelope play,
> Where seldom is heard a discouraging word
> and the skies are not cloudy all day.
> Home, home on the range,
> Where the deer and the antelope play
> Where seldom is heard a discouraging word
> and the skies are not cloudy all day.

POPULATION

Population: 2,364,236, thirty-second among the states

Population Density: 29 persons per sq. mi. (11 persons per km²)

Population Distribution: 66 percent of the people live in cities or towns. Wichita, Kansas City, and Topeka are the state's major cities.

Wichita	279,835
Kansas City	161,087
Topeka	115,266
Overland Park	81,784
Lawrence	52,738
Salina	41,843
Hutchinson	40,284
Olathe	37,258
Leavenworth	33,656
Manhattan	32,644

(Population figures according to 1980 census)

Population Growth: Settlers seeking fertile land streamed into Kansas in the years before statehood. They flooded the state after 1862, when the Homestead Act offered land at bargain prices. The Kansas migration slowed by 1890. Since then, growth has been steady but slow, and lower than the national average.

Year	Population
1860	107,206
1880	996,296
1900	1,470,495
1920	1,769,257
1940	1,801,028
1950	1,905,299
1960	2,178,611
1970	2,249,071
1980	2,364,236

GEOGRAPHY

Borders: States that border Kansas include Nebraska on the north, Missouri on the east, Oklahoma on the south, and Colorado on the west.

Highest Point: Mount Sunflower in Wallace County, 4,039 ft. (1,231 m)

Lowest Point: Verdigris River in Montgomery County, 680 ft. (207 m)

**Monument Rocks
National Landmark**

Greatest Distances: North to south—206 mi. (332 km)
East to west—408 mi. (657 km)

Area: 82,277 sq. mi. (213,097 km²)

Rank in Area Among the States: Fourteenth

Rivers: Kansas lies entirely within the Mississippi River's drainage area. All of
the state's important rivers flow directly or indirectly into the Mississippi. The
Missouri River, America's longest river, forms a small part of the state's
northeastern border. It joins with the Kansas River at Kansas City. The Republican
and Smoky Hill rivers unite at Manhattan to form the Kansas River. Another major
river, the Arkansas, flows through the southern and western part of the state.
Western Kansas has many rivers and creeks. Most of them are broad and shallow.

Lakes: Most Kansas lakes are artificial reservoirs formed by damming the state's
rivers. Milford Lake on the Republican River, which covers about 16,000 acres
(6,475 hectares), is the largest such lake. Other large lakes include Wilson Lake,
Tuttle Creek Lake, Cheney Reservoir, Elk City Lake, Perry Lake, and John
Redmond Reservoir.

Topography: Geographers divide Kansas into four main regions: the High Plains, Plains Border (both of which are part of the Great Plains region), Southeastern Plains (which include the Flint Hills and the Osage Plains), and Dissected Till Plains.

The High Plains, occupying the western third of the state, appear to be flat and treeless, though they are actually punctuated by valleys, ravines, arroyos, and canyons. Some of Kansas's most interesting geological formations are found in this region. The Plains Border region, occupying the middle third of the state, contains hills and uplands, plus occasional dunes, chalk beds, and rock formations. The Flint Hills region of east-central Kansas, named for its abundant limestone ridges, is a rolling, mainly treeless area. Covered by bluestem grasses, it is one of the world's best grazing areas. The Osage Plains region, in the southeastern part of the state, is characterized by a series of low, rolling hills. Rich soils left by advancing and receding glaciers are the most notable feature of the northeastern Dissected Till Plains. It is a hilly, forested area that has many creeks and springs.

Climate: Kansas, like most other Great Plains states, has a generally moderate climate, with an average annual temperature of 55° F. (13° C), though extremes in temperature are experienced in winter and summer. Temperatures in Wichita generally range from 23° F. to 41° F. (-5° C to 5° C) in January and from 69° F. to 92° F. (21° C to 33° C) in July. Topeka temperatures vary from 19° F. to 39° F. (-7° C to 4° C) in January and 68° F. to 91° F. (20° C to 33° C) in July. The highest recorded temperature in Kansas history was 121° F. (49° C), at Fredonia on July 18, 1936; and near Alton six days later. The thermometer plunged to a record -40° F. (-40° C) at Lebanon on February 13, 1905. The state is known for its abundance of clear days; the sun shines more than 275 days a year in Kansas. The state receives an average of 27 in. (69 cm) of precipitation annually. Blizzards may sweep into the state from the north in wintertime. Tornadoes, droughts, and floods occur periodically.

NATURE

Trees: Ash, cottonwood, black walnut, pecan, hickory, elm, hackberry, sycamore, willow, maple, oak, dogwood, locust, red cedar, box elder

Wild Plants: Russian thistle (tumbleweed), sunflower, aster, clover, ragwort, columbine, daisy, goldenrod, thistle, verbena, morning glory, osage orange, primrose, prairie phlox, prickly pear, yucca, may apple, wild indigo, many kinds of grasses

Animals: Buffalo, deer, antelope, coyote, muskrat, opossum, prairie dog, rabbit, raccoon, bear, skunk, mink, rattlesnake, beavers, badger, fox

Birds: Western meadowlark, hawk, blue jay, cardinal, robin, sparrow, owl, woodpecker, partridge, goose, pheasant, prairie chicken, quail, wild turkey

Fish: Bass, bluegill, catfish, crappie, carp, walleye

Great horned owls (left) and prairie dogs (right) are among the many kinds of animals found in Kansas.

GOVERNMENT

Kansas is governed under its original constitution, although that document has been amended more than 75 times. Amendments may be made by approval of two-thirds of both houses of the state legislature, plus a majority of statewide voters. A constitutional convention may be called if approved by two-thirds of the members of both houses and a majority of voters.

Government in Kansas, like the federal government, is divided into three branches. The legislative branch, which makes the laws, consists of a 40-member senate and a 125-member house of representatives. Senators are elected to four-year terms; representatives to two-year terms.

The governor heads the executive branch, which enforces the laws. Other executive branch officials include the lieutenant governor, secretary of state, treasurer, attorney general, and commissioner of insurance. All are elected to four-year terms. The governor and lieutenant governor may serve an unlimited number of terms, but no more than two consecutive terms.

At the top of the state's judicial branch is the supreme court, whose seven justices are elected to six-year terms. New justices are appointed by the governor from a list given to him by a supreme court nominating commission. After a year, voters decide whether to retain the new judge. The supreme court judge with the longest tenure serves as chief justice. Kansas has a court of appeals made up of seven members elected to four-year terms. The state also has district courts, whose judges are elected to four-year terms.

Number of Counties: 105

113

Fort Hays State University

U.S. Representatives: 5

Electoral Votes: 7

Voting Qualifications: U.S. citizen, 18 years of age, resident of the state 20 days before election

EDUCATION

Early missionaries established the first Kansas schools, which were set up to educate and convert the region's Indians. When white settlers began inhabiting Kansas, schools immediately followed. The state constitution, drawn up in 1859, provided for a system of elementary, secondary, and higher education.

Children in Kansas must attend school from ages seven to sixteen. Kansas has about 282,000 elementary and 124,000 secondary-school students. Annually, the state spends about $3,361 per student, slightly above the national average.

The University of Kansas at Lawrence and Kansas State University at Manhattan, members of the prestigious Big Eight conference, are the largest state colleges. Other state-run schools include Wichita State University in Wichita, Emporia State University in Emporia, Fort Hays State University in Hays, and Pittsburg State University in Pittsburg. Private schools include Baker University in Baldwin City,

Benedictine College in Atchison, Bethany College in Lindsborg, Central Baptist Theological Seminary in Seminary Heights, Bethel College in North Newton, Friends University and Kansas Newman College in Wichita, Kansas Wesleyan and Marymount College in Salina, McPherson College in McPherson, Mid-America Nazarene College in Olathe, Ottawa University in Ottawa, St. Mary College in Leavenworth, St. Mary of the Plains College in Dodge City, Southwestern College in Winfield, Sterling College in Sterling, Tabor College in Hillsboro, Washburn University of Topeka in Topeka, and the U.S. Army Command and General Staff College in Fort Leavenworth.

ECONOMY AND INDUSTRY

Principal Products:
Agriculture: Wheat, sorghum, corn, sheep, beef cattle, dairy products, poultry, soybeans, hogs, sugar beets, flax, fruit, rye, oats, alfalfa, barley, apples
Manufacturing: Machinery, petroleum refining, aircraft, transportation equipment, food products, chemicals, printed materials, plastic products
Natural Resources: Oil, natural gas, salt, coal, helium, gypsum, lead, zinc, stone, gravel

Business and Trade: Transportation equipment provides a large share of Kansas's important manufacturing economy. Wichita factories build more than half of the civilian aircraft made in the United States. Salina, Wellington, and Winfield also manufacture airplane parts. Kansas City has a large automobile manufacturing plant, and rubber tires are made in Topeka. Atchison, Wichita, Junction City, and Topeka are centers for the manufacture of railroad equipment. Kansas also produces food products, printed materials, nonelectrical machinery, and chemicals.

Kansas also extracts wealth from the earth. Natural gas deposits in the southwestern part of the state, coal deposits in the southeast, and oil in central Kansas provide much of that wealth. Kansas is one of the nation's leading producers of helium. The Hutchinson area has a huge salt deposit. Other mineral resources include lead, zinc, cement, sand, and gravel.

Wichita, Kansas City, Topeka, Hutchinson, and Salina—all early railroad centers—are the state's most important trading cities. Kansas City, because of its location on the Missouri River, is also a river port.

Communication: In 1835, missionary Jotham Meeker began publishing the *Shawnee Sun,* a monthly newspaper in the Shawnee language. It was the state's first newspaper, and the first Indian language periodical in the United States. Twenty years later, the *Kansas Weekly Herald* in Fort Leavenworth became the state's first regular weekly paper. Through the years Kansas has produced many notable papers, including the Emporia *Gazette,* published by famed editor William Allen White. Today, Kansas has about 250 newspapers, including about 50 dailies. The *Wichita Eagle-Beacon* has the largest circulation. Other important Kansas newspapers include the *Capital-Journal* of Topeka, the *Hutchinson News,* and the *Salina Journal.*

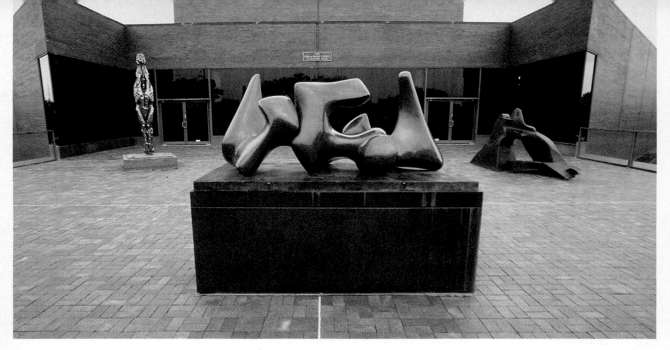

American art from colonial times to the present is featured at the Wichita Art Museum.

Kansas radio broadcasting began in 1922 with KFH in Wichita. Now Kansas has about 125 radio stations. WQKAK at Kansas State College (now Kansas State University) received one of the first television licenses in America. The state's first commercial station, KTVH in Hutchinson, started operation in 1953. Today, Kansans are served by about 20 television stations.

Transportation: Railroads and river traffic along the Missouri provided the first forms of transportation in Kansas. Wagon trains also crossed Kansas, most of them merely passing through on their way west.

Kansas, because of its central location, is still an important link in the nation's transportation system. Ranked fifth among the states in railroad mileage, Kansas is crossed by about 7,000 mi. (11,265 km) of railroad track. Fourteen railroads provide freight service, and passenger trains stop in about a dozen cities.

More than 132,000 mi. (212,428 km) of roads and highways cross the state. These include several interstate routes. I-70, which runs through Kansas City and Topeka, is a major east-west route across the state. I-35, the Kansas Turnpike, connects Topeka and Wichita. Kansas has about 370 airports, including abut 125 public ones. Six airlines serve twelve cities in the state.

SOCIAL AND CULTURAL LIFE

Museums: Kansas is proud of its educational and cultural heritage, and that pride shows in the state's many museums. The Wichita Art Museum features American art and the works of "cowboy artist" Charles M. Russell. The Helen F. Spencer Museum of Art, at the University of Kansas in Lawrence, has the state's most comprehensive collection of art. Lawrence Art Center, in Lawrence, has galleries dedicated to local artists. Other fine art museums include the Edwin A.

Century II, a cultural and convention center in Wichita

Ulrich Museum of Art, at Wichita State University; and the Mulvane Art Museum, at Washburn University in Topeka. The Birger Sandzen Memorial Gallery in Lindsborg celebrates the work of noted Minnesota artist Birger Sandzen.

Kansas also has a wealth of science museums. The Kansas Cosmosphere and Space Center in Hutchinson is one of the nation's most important space centers. The Omnisphere and Science Center in Wichita features a planetarium and a hands-on science center. The Kansas Health Museum in Halstead features exhibits on health care and the workings of the human body. The Museum of Anthropology at the University of Kansas contains artifacts from the Americas, Africa, Australia, and New Guinea. Those interested in insects can also visit the university's Snow Entomological Museum. Thompson Hall at Kansas State University boasts many rare rocks and minerals. Fick Fossil and History Museum in Oakley has fossils, rocks, minerals, and a shark's-tooth collection, plus a sod house and replica of a train depot. Fossil Station Museum in Russell describes the history of oil rock. Dyche Museum of Natural History at the University of Kansas is the state's largest natural-history museum.

The state's largest historical museum, the Kansas Museum of History in Topeka, offers thousands of exhibits relating to the history of Kansas. Among the many other fine historical museums in the state are the Wichita Sedgwick County Historical Museum; the Pawnee Indian Village Museum near Belleville, built near the site of a Pawnee village; the Coronado Museum in Liberal, which traces the Spanish explorer's route through Kansas; the Pony Express Barn Museum in

117

Marysville; and the High Plains Museum in Goodland, which displays Indian artifacts, farm machinery, and household items.

Libraries: The first Kansas library opened at Vinland in 1859. Today the state has more than three hundred libraries in seven regional systems. Watson Memorial Library, at the University of Kansas, is the state's largest library. The library of the Kansas State Historical Society in Topeka includes collections on the history of American Indians, Kansas, and the West, as well as one of the largest newspaper collections in the nation. The Emporia Public Library holds a valuable collection of city directories, newspapers dating from 1857, and a complete file of the Emporia *Gazette*. President Dwight D. Eisenhower's papers are housed at the Dwight D. Eisenhower Library in Abilene. Baker University's library houses the Bishop Quayle Bible Collection.

Performing Arts: Brown Grand Opera House in Concordia, a restored 1907 opera house, presents plays, concerts, shows, and ballets. Lawrence Art Center is a performance hall for theater, dance, and music. Century II, in Wichita, is a large convention center that also houses a theater and concert hall. Lindsborg holds an annual Messiah Festival that features oratorios of Handel and Bach. Winfield hosts the Walnut Valley Bluegrass Festival each year. The Kansas Folklife Festival in Manhattan honors the state's traditional arts and artists. Topeka and Wichita both support symphony orchestras.

Sports and Recreation: Jayhawkers from Kansas City to Elkhart celebrated in 1988 when the University of Kansas Jayhawks won the NCAA college basketball tournament. The Jayhawks are not the only college basketball power in the state, however, as Kansas State and Wichita State supporters will attest. Soccer is also an important sport in Kansas. The Wichita Wings are perennial contenders in the Major Indoor Soccer League. Some baseball and football fans root for the Kansas City Royals and Kansas City Chiefs of nearby Kansas City, Missouri. Outdoors enthusiasts enjoy hunting, fishing, and camping at Kansas's 23 state parks and 40 state lakes.

Historic Sites and Landmarks:

Barton County Historical Village and Museum, in Great Bend, contains a church, schoolhouse, agricultural buildings, homestead and post office from the late 1800s and early 1900s.

John Brown Memorial State Park, in Osawatomie, preserves the cabins and furnishings of the famed abolitionist.

El Cuartelejo, near Scott City, was an Indian pueblo occupied by the Picuris tribe from 1650 to 1720.

Fort Hays, in Hays, was built in 1865 to protect military roads, guard the mails, and defend the men constructing the Union Pacific Railroad. Its original blockhouse, guardhouse, and officers' quarters have been restored.

A Civil War reenactment at Fort Scott National Historic Site

Fort Larned National Historic Site, near Larned, is a restored post, built in 1859 to protect travelers on the Santa Fe Trail, that includes officers' quarters, barracks, a blacksmith shop, and a post office. The site is administered by the National Park Service.

Fort Leavenworth, built in 1827 and still an active military post, is the oldest post in continuous operation west of the Mississippi River. It features several historic structures, a national cemetery, branches of the Oregon and Santa Fe Trails, and the Post Museum, which holds the nation's largest collection of horse-drawn vehicles.

Fort Riley, near Junction City, was the home of the U.S. Cavalry during much of its existence. On the grounds are the Custer House, the 1854 home of famous General George Custer; Kansas's first territorial capitol; and the U.S. Cavalry Museum.

Fort Scott National Historic Site, in Fort Scott, is the site of an 1842 military post established to keep peace on the Indian frontier. It features twenty buildings restored by the National Park Service, as well as National Cemetery Number One.

Historic Front Street, in Dodge City, is a reconstruction of two blocks of the street as it appeared in the 1870s, and includes an accredited museum of the Old West.

Near Independence is a replica of the log cabin lived in and described by Laura Ingalls Wilder in her autobiographical book *Little House on the Prairie*.

Shawnee Methodist Mission, in Kansas City, served as an Indian school from 1830 to 1862.

Other Interesting Places to Visit:

Bartlett Arboretum, near Wellington, contains flowers, ornamental grasses, shrubs, and trees from around the world.

Cedar Crest Governor's Mansion, in Topeka, is a Norman-style château that was built in 1928 and has been the home of Kansas's chief executives since 1962.

Eisenhower Center, in Abilene, honors the Kansas son who became the nation's thirty-fourth president. It includes the Eisenhower Museum, the Dwight D. Eisenhower Library, the Eisenhower family home, and the final resting place of Dwight and Mamie Eisenhower.

Gallery of Also Rans, in Norton, honors unsuccessful presidential candidates.

Grain Elevator, in Hutchinson, is the world's longest grain-storage building.

Hall of Generals, in Abilene, is a wax museum honoring famous generals who served under Dwight D. Eisenhower.

Visitors can learn about the "cowtown" era at Old Abilene Town in Abilene.

Hays House, in Council Grove, is said to be the oldest continuously operating restaurant west of the Mississippi River.

Huron Indian Cemetery, in Kansas City, is a burial ground that was used by the Wyandotte Indians between 1844 and 1959.

International Forest of Friendship, in Atchison, contains trees from all fifty states, as well as thirty-three countries.

Kansas State Fish Hatchery, in Pratt, has more than ninety brood ponds, plus a museum and aquarium.

Little House on the Prairie, near Independence, is a replica of the log cabin once lived in by author Laura Ingalls Wilder.

Mid-America All-Indian Center and Museum, in Wichita, explores North America's Native American heritage through exhibits of traditional and contemporary works from the Plains, Southwest, Northwest Coast, and Eskimo cultural areas.

Old Abilene Town, a replica of Abilene during the cattle boom, includes original buildings and stagecoach rides.

Red Rocks, in Emporia, was the home of famed newspaper publisher William Allen White.

State Capitol, in Topeka, is a French Renaissance building that was completed in 1903. Built of native limestone and modeled after the U.S. Capitol, it contains murals by famous Kansas-born artist John Steuart Curry.

IMPORTANT DATES

12,000-5000 B.C.—First native Americans arrive in Kansas

A.D. 1000-1500—Indians known to scholars as the Village Farmers domesticate plants in Kansas

1541—Spanish explorer Francisco Vásquez de Coronado becomes the first European to visit Kansas

c. 1650-1720—Picuris Indians occupy El Cuartelejo

1724—French fur trader Étienne de Bourgmont travels through present-day Kansas

1803—U.S. acquires most of present-day Kansas in Louisiana Purchase

1804—Lewis and Clark expedition passes through Kansas on its way to the Pacific Ocean

1806—Zebulon Pike crosses present-day Kansas on his way west

1820—Missouri Compromise prohibits slavery in the land that is now Kansas

1821—William Becknell establishes Santa Fe Trail, much of which runs through Kansas

1825—Osage Indians sign a treaty with U.S. government guaranteeing safe passage for those traveling through Kansas on the Santa Fe Trail; a federal law calls for removal of eastern Indians to lands west of Missouri and Arkansas; over the next fifteen years, nearly thirty different groups settle in Kansas, including the Shawnee, Delaware, Wyandot, Miami, Ottawa, Pottawatomie, Kickapoo, Chippewa, Iowa, Sac, and Fox

1827—Fort Leavenworth, the first permanent white settlement in Kansas, is established

1830—The Reverend Thomas Johnson founds Shawnee Methodist Mission in present-day Wyandotte County

1831—Moses Grinter establishes the first ferry across the Kansas River; Isaac McCoy founds Shawnee Baptist Mission

1835—Baptist missionary Jotham Meeker publishes the *Shawnee Sun*, Kansas's first newspaper and the first in the nation to be published in an Indian language

1844—Senator Stephen A. Douglas introduces first bill to organize Kansas territory

1853—Some 13 million acres (5.3 million hectares) of Kansas land that had been promised to the Indians "forever" is reclaimed by the U.S. government, forcing Indians living in Kansas to move southward into present-day Oklahoma

1854—Kansas-Nebraska Act opens Kansas lands to white settlers, creates the Kansas Territory, and provides that settlers will decide whether Kansas will allow or prohibit slavery, setting off years of "Bleeding Kansas" skirmishes between proslavery and antislavery groups

1855—Territorial legislature provides for a system of public schools

1856—Proslavery "Border Ruffians" virtually destroy the town of Lawrence; antislavery zealot John Brown kills five proslavery settlers

1858—Border Ruffians kill five free-staters in Marais des Cygnes

1859—A telegraph union, the first labor association in Kansas, opens; Fort Larned is built to protect travelers; first library in Kansas is established in Vinland

1860—U.S. House of Representatives votes to admit Kansas as a free state, but the Senate rejects the vote; Republican Abraham Lincoln campaigns to admit Kansas as a free state

1861—Kansas enters the Union as the thirty-fourth state

1862—Homestead Act opens up Kansas land at low prices

1863—Confederate raiders led by William Quantrill kill more than 150 persons during an attack on Lawrence

1867—U.S. government negotiates treaty with five Plains Indians tribes near Medicine Lodge; Union Pacific Railroad arrives at Abilene, which becomes the terminus of the Chisholm Trail

1868—Wichita is founded

1872—Railroads reach Dodge City

1873—Russian Mennonites begin settling in Kansas; they introduce to Kansas Turkey Red, a hardy, drought-resistant wheat

1874—An invasion of grasshoppers forces many newly arrived settlers to leave the state

1880—Kansas becomes the first state to have constitutional prohibition

1884—Haskell Institute (now Haskell Indian Junior College) is founded to educate Indians

1886—A terrible blizzard kills some 20 percent of the state's cattle herds

1887—Women receive voting rights in municipal elections; Susanna Salter of Argonia becomes the nation's first woman mayor

1890—People's party (Populist party) organizes in Kansas

1892—Dalton Gang attempts a bank robbery at Coffeyville; oil is discovered at Neodesha

1893—"Legislative War of 1893" takes place, and both Republicans and Populists claim majority in state house of representatives

1900—Carry Nation begins her campaign against saloons

1903—Work is completed on present state capitol; drillers discover the nation's first helium deposits, at Dexter

1912—A state constitutional amendment grants women full suffrage

1915—El Dorado Pool in Butler County, the state's first large oil field, opens

1923—Emporia *Gazette* editor and publisher William Allen White wins the first of his two Pulitzer Prizes

1934-35—Dust Bowl conditions devastate Kansas farmers

1936—Governor Alf Landon wins Republican nomination for president, but loses to Franklin D. Roosevelt

1937—Kansas establishes a state department of social welfare

1939—*The Wizard of Oz*, a film that makes Kansas famous throughout the world, premieres

1941-45—Kansas's aircraft industry expands during World War II

1952—Kansas native Dwight D. Eisenhower is elected president

1953—Kansas native William Inge wins Pulitzer Prize for the play *Picnic*

1954—In the landmark case *Brown vs. Board of Education of Topeka*, the U.S. Supreme Court outlaws segregation in public schools

1958—Kansas approves a right-to-work law

1962—State legislature establishes a statewide system of vocational schools

1963—Many smaller schools are consolidated to make better use of school funds

1965—State legislature provides for a system of junior colleges

1971—Kansas native Earl Sutherland wins a Nobel Prize in Physiology or Medicine for his work with hormones

1972—A constitutional amendment increases the governor's term from two to four years

1976—Kansas native Robert Dole wins the Rupublican nomination for vice-president, but the Gerald Ford-Dole ticket loses the presidential election to Jimmy Carter

1978—Nancy Landon Kassebaum, daughter of Alf Landon, becomes the first woman U.S. senator from Kansas and the first woman elected to a full term in the Senate who did not succeed her husband

1985—Robert Dole becomes Senate majority leader

1988—University of Kansas wins NCAA basketball championship

IMPORTANT PEOPLE

Hugh Beaumont (1909-1982), born in Lawrence; actor; starred as a kindly, all-knowing father in classic television series "Leave It to Beaver"

Gwendolyn Brooks (1917-   ), born in Topeka; poet; used short, rapid verses to describe the plight of poor blacks; won 1950 Pulitzer Prize in poetry for *Annie Allen*; other famous works include *A Street in Bronzeville* and *Report from Part One*

Earl Russell Browder (1891-1973), born in Wichita; politician; longtime leader of the American Communist party; Communist party candidate for president in 1936 and 1940

GWENDOLYN BROOKS

JOHN BROWN

WALTER CHRYSLER

WILLIAM CODY

CHARLES CURTIS

John Brown (1800-1859), abolitionist; thought it necessary to use violent means to end slavery; worked to keep Kansas from becoming a slave state by attacking proslavery settlers; raided U.S. arsenal at Harpers Ferry, Virginia, in order to start a general slave rebellion; was convicted of treason and hanged

Wilt Chamberlain (1936-   ); professional basketball player; starred at center for University of Kansas Jayhawks; one of the greatest scorers in NBA history; scored 100 points in one game in 1962; averaged 50.4 points in 1961-1962 season; led NBA in scoring seven consecutive times; led great Philadelphia 76ers and Los Angeles Lakers teams to NBA titles

Walter Percy Chrysler (1875-1940), born in Wamego; industrialist; founded Chrysler Corporation and built it into the nation's third-largest automobile company; built Chrysler Building (at that time the world's tallest building) in New York City (1929)

Clark McAdams Clifford (1906-   ), born in Fort Scott; public official; U.S. secretary of defense under President Lyndon Johnson (1968-69); worked to diminish U.S. involvement in Vietnam War by transferring burden of fighting from American to Vietnamese forces

William Frederick "Buffalo Bill" Cody (1846-1917), scout, explorer, entertainer; scouted for U.S. Army and led buffalo hunting expeditions; Pony Express rider (1860); scout for Kansas cavalry against Indians (1863); organized and appeared in a famous Wild West show that toured U.S. and Europe (1883-1916)

Francisco Vásquez de Coronado (1510-1554), Spanish explorer; became first known European to explore present-day Kansas (1541)

Glenn Cunningham (1909-1988), born in Elkhart; track and field athlete; survived burns from a childhood fire to become one of the greatest runners in history; won NCAA and AAU championships; received Sullivan Trophy for outstanding athletics; set world record in 1,500-meter event at 1936 Olympics

John Steuart Curry (1897-1946), born in Dunavant; artist; led the "Regionalist" school of American painters who used a simple, straightforward style and concentrated on scenes of everyday American life; was inspired by Kansas in such works as *Tornado Over Kansas*, *Baptism in Kansas*, *Spring Shower*, and *The Gospel Train*; painted murals for Kansas State Capitol in Topeka, and U.S. Department of Justice and Department of Interior buildings in Washington, D.C.

Charles Curtis (1860-1936), born in North Topeka (now Topeka); politician; U.S. representative from Kansas (1893-1907); U.S. senator (1907-13, 1915-29); Senate majority leader (1925-29); U.S. vice-president under Herbert Hoover (1929-33); first person of Native American ancestry (his mother was part Kaw) to achieve that office

Elwood "Bingo" De Moss (1899-1965), born in Topeka; professional baseball player; starred for early Negro League baseball teams; was considered by many to be the greatest second baseman of his time; led Chicago American Giants to four championships

Robert Joseph Dole (1923-   ), born in Russell; politician; U.S. representative from Kansas (1961-68); U.S. senator (1969-   ); Republican nominee for vice-president (1976); chairman of Senate Finance Committee (1981-87); Senate majority leader (1985-87); Senate minority leader (1987-   ); helped sponsor food-stamp program and a bill to make Martin Luther King, Jr.'s birthday a national holiday; preserved Voting Rights Act; advocated programs for the disabled

ROBERT DOLE

Amelia Mary Earhart (1898-1937?), born in Atchison; aviator; first woman to make a solo flight across the Atlantic Ocean (1932); disappeared while attempting a round-the-world flight

Wyatt Earp (1848-1929), law officer; kept the peace in Kansas cowtowns; assistant marshal of Dodge City (1876, 1878-79); while deputy marshal of Tombstone, Arizona, fought classic Western gunfight at the O.K. Corral (1881)

AMELIA EARHART

Dwight David Eisenhower (1890-1969), grew up in Abilene; thirty-fourth president of the U.S. (1953-61); supreme commander of Allied forces in Europe during World War II; planned and commanded D-Day invasion of Europe (June 6, 1944); chief of staff of U.S. Army (1945-48); president of Columbia University (1948-53); supreme commander of NATO forces in Europe (1951-52); as president, signed truce ending Korean War (1953), ended the Suez crisis (1956), sent National Guard troops to Little Rock, Arkansas, to enforce desegregation of its public high school (1957), launched the space program, and severed diplomatic relations with Cuba (1961)

WYATT EARP

Milton Eisenhower (1899-1985), born in Abilene; educator, public official; brother of Dwight Eisenhower; headed Office of War Information during World War II; president of Kansas State University (1943-50), Pennsylvania State University (1950-56), and Johns Hopkins University (1956-67, 1971-72)

Dorothy Canfield Fisher (1879-1958), born in Lawrence; novelist; in her books, explored the lives of middle-class women; best-known works include *The Squirrel Cage, A Brimming Cup, Her Son's Wife,* and *The Deepening Stream*

Robert Merrell Gage (1892-   ), born in Topeka; sculptor; created *Pioneer Woman of Kansas,* a kneeling woman holding a rifle and sheltering her children; designed a statue of Abraham Lincoln that is located on state capitol grounds

MILTON EISENHOWER

GEORGIA GRAY

EDWARD HOCH

WILLIAM INGE

WALTER JOHNSON

Georgia Neese Clark Gray (1900-   ), born in Richland; public official; U.S. treasurer (1949-53)

Gary Hart (1936-   ), born in Ottawa; politician; directed George McGovern's presidential campaign in 1972; U.S. senator from Colorado (1975-87)

James Butler "Wild Bill" Hickok (1837-1876), scout, law officer; Union scout and guerrilla fighter; deputy U.S. marshal of Fort Riley (1866-67); U.S. marshal of Hays City (1869-71) and Abilene (1871); died while gambling in a Deadwood, South Dakota, saloon

Edward Hoch (1849-1925); politician; governor of Kansas (1905-09); as governor, worked to rid Kansas of "bossism"

Cyrus Holliday (1826-1900); industrialist; founded Atchison, Topeka, & Santa Fe Railroad

Dennis Hopper (1936-   ), born in Dodge City; actor, director; starred in, wrote, and directed the antiestablishment film *Easy Rider*; directed the controversial film *Colors*; appeared in *Rebel without a Cause* and *The Osterman Weekend*

Edgar Watson Howe (1853-1937); publisher, novelist; edited *Atchison Globe*, which became a powerful force in Kansas politics; wrote *The Story of a Country Town*, a novel that explored small-town life

Langston Hughes (1902-1967), grew up in Lawrence; poet, novelist; one of the leading black poets of the 1920s and 1930s; his novel *Not Without Laughter* describes his youth in Kansas

John James Ingalls (1833-1900); editor, lawyer, politician; helped found *Kansas Magazine*; U.S. senator from Kansas (1873-91); known for his writing and oratory skills

William Inge (1913-1973), born in Independence; novelist, playwright; wrote intense stories and plays about people in small towns; won 1953 Pulitzer Prize in drama for *Picnic*; also wrote the plays *Bus Stop* and *The Dark at the Top of the Stairs*

Hugh S. Johnson (1882-1942), born in Fort Scott; soldier, public official; directed selective service program during World War I; headed National Recovery Administration during "New Deal" years of Franklin D. Roosevelt's presidency

Walter "Big Train" Johnson (1887-1946), born in Humboldt; professional baseball player; won 416 major-league games for Washington Senators, more than any other pitcher in American League history; threw 110 shutouts, the most ever in the major leagues; led American League in strikeouts 11 times; considered by many to be the greatest pitcher of all time; elected to Baseball Hall of Fame (1936)

Nancy Landon Kassebaum (1932-   ), born in Topeka; politician; first woman U.S. senator from Kansas (1979-   ); worked to improve Senate's efficiency in doing business; worked closely with Democrats to attain workable budgets

NANCY KASSEBAUM

Buster Keaton (1895-1966), born Joseph Frank Keaton in Piqua; stone-faced comedian who starred in such silent films as *The General, The Navigator,* and *The Cameraman*

Emmett Kelly (1898-1979), born in Sedan; clown; appeared with Ringling Brothers, Barnum & Bailey Circus; created "Weary Willy," a sad-faced hobo always defeated by life's little problems

Stan Kenton (1912-1979), born in Wichita; musician; played piano and led jazz bands ranging from small combos to big bands; combined jazz and Afro-Cuban rhythms; composed "Artistry in Rhythm" and "Eager Beaver"

BUSTER KEATON

Ronald (Ron) Kramer (1935-   ), born in Girard; professional football player; starred as tight end for Vince Lombardi's great Green Bay Packer teams; helped lead Packers to NFL championships in 1961 and 1962

Alfred Mossman (Alf) Landon (1887-1987); politician; governor of Kansas (1933-37); as governor, won a reputation for modernization, economy, and budget-balancing; was Republican presidential nominee in 1936, but lost landslide election to Franklin Delano Roosevelt; in later years, won affection as a Republican elder statesman

James Henry Lane (1814-1866), born in Lawrenceburg; soldier, politician; helped lead Kansas "Free State" movement; commanded an "army" of irregulars who raided proslavery districts in Kansas (1856); U.S. senator from Kansas (1861-66); assumed rank of brigadier general during Civil War

EMMETT KELLY

Edgar Lee Masters (1868-1950), born in Garnett; poet; most famous work is *Spoon River Anthology,* about residents of a mythical small midwestern town

William Barclay (Bat) Masterson (1853-1921), law officer, editor; moved to Kansas in 1870 and became known as a scout, Indian fighter, and gambler; sheriff of Ford County (1877); colorful figure of the Old West who was known for upholding the law and keeping peace on the frontier; wore fancy clothes and carried a trademark cane; sports editor of the New York City *Morning Telegraph* (1902-21)

Joseph McCoy (1837-1915); rancher; brought first cattle herds to Abilene for shipment to Chicago, helping Abilene become a famous cowtown

Hattie McDaniel (1895-1952), born in Wichita; actress; won the 1939 Academy Award for best supporting actress for her role as Mammy in *Gone With the Wind*

EDGAR LEE MASTERS

KARL MENNINGER

CARRY NATION

ZASU PITTS

DAMON RUNYON

Karl Augustus (1893-1990) and **William Claire** (1899-1966) **Menninger**, both born in Topeka; psychiatrists; with their father, **Charles F. Menninger** (1862-1953), founded Menninger Clinic and Menninger Foundation in Topeka, one of the world's leading psychiatric centers

James A. Naismith (1861-1939); educator, invented the game of basketball (1891); taught physical education at the University of Kansas in his later years

Carry A. Nation (1846-1911), temperance leader; settled in Kansas in 1889; in 1900, as part of her crusade against alcoholic beverages, began using a hatchet to destroy saloons in major Kansas cities

Charlie "Bird" Parker (1920-1955), born in Kansas City; saxophonist, composer; popularized bebop jazz of 1940s; among his many famous pieces are "Ornithology" and "Confirmation"

Gordon Alexander Buchanan Parks (1912-   ), born in Fort Scott; photographer, director, author, composer; won awards as a photographer for *Life* magazine; produced, directed, and wrote the films *Shaft* and *The Learning Tree*; composed piano concertos and sonatas

ZaSu Pitts (1898-1963), born in Parsons; actress; played flighty, absent-minded friends of leading ladies; appeared in the television program "The Gale Storm Show"

Marvin Rainwater (1925-   ), born in Wichita; country singer; performed in traditional Indian dress; recorded "Gonna Find Me a Bluebird"

John Riggins (1949-   ), born in Centralia; professional football player; ran for 11,352 yards with New York Jets and Washington Redskins; broke University of Kansas rushing records held by Gale Sayers

Charles Robinson (1818-1894); physician, politician, abolitionist; leader of Kansas's "free-state" movement; elected territorial governor by the free-state faction (1856); first governor of the state of Kansas (1861-63)

Charles (Buddy) Rogers (1904-   ), born in Olathe; actor; starred in *Wings*, the first motion picture to win an Academy Award

Edmund Gibson Ross (1826-1907); politician; led free-state settlers to Kansas (1856); U.S. senator from Kansas (1866-71); in 1868, cast the deciding vote—against conviction—during the impeachment trial of President Andrew Johnson; this action ruined his political career in Kansas but earned him a reputation for political courage; territorial governor of New Mexico (1885-89)

Damon Runyon (1880-1946), born in Manhattan; author; described exploits of colorful, lowlife characters; wrote *Guys and Dolls, Blue Plate Special,* and *Take It Easy*

James Ronald (Jim) Ryun (1947-   ), born in Wichita; track and field athlete; set a world record for the mile in 1967; won silver medal in 1968 Olympics

Susanna M. Salter (1860-1961); politician; became first woman mayor in the U.S. when elected mayor of Argonia in 1887

Sven Birger Sandzen (1871-1954); artist, teacher; specialized in prairie scenes painted in impressionistic technique; taught at Bethany College in Lindsborg, which he helped make into a midwestern art center

Gale Eugene Sayers (1943-   ), born in Wichita; professional football player; known as the "Kansas Comet" for his swift running while at University of Kansas; scored six touchdowns in one game for Chicago Bears; was named the greatest running back in the National Football League's first half century

Jeremiah Simpson (1842-1905); politician; nicknamed "Sockless Jerry"; came to Kansas and became a cattle rancher (1884); entered politics as a Populist; U.S. representative from Kansas (1891-95, 1897-99)

Paul Starrett (1866-1957), born in Lawrence; building contractor; was responsible for erecting such famous New York City buildings as the Flatiron Building (1922) and the Empire State Building (1931)

Earl Sutherland (1915-1974), born in Burlingame; scientist; won 1971 Nobel Prize in Physiology and Medicine for his work on the mechanisms of hormones

John Cameron Swayze (1906-   ), born in Wichita; journalist; became television's first superstar anchorman, with "Camel News Caravan"

Joseph Bert Tinker (1880-1948), born in Muscotah; professional baseball player; played shortstop in famous "Tinker to Evers to Chance" Chicago Cubs infield; led Cubs to four National League pennants and two world championships; elected to Baseball Hall of Fame (1946)

Clyde Tombaugh (1906-   ), astronomer; studied astronomy at the University of Kansas; discovered the planet Pluto in 1930

Vivian Vance (1912-1979), born in Cherryville; actress; starred as Lucille Ball's friend and neighbor Ethel Mertz in the famed television series "I Love Lucy"

Bernard Warkentin (1847-1908); agriculturalist; revolutionized state's economy by introducing hardy Turkey Red winter wheat; enabled Kansas to earn reputation as the "Wheat State"

Paul Wellman (1895-1966), lived in Kansas; reporter, author; wrote twenty-three books, including *Walls of Jericho* and *The Chain*; wrote screenplays, including *The Comancheros* and *The Iron Mistress*

SUSANNA SALTER

GALE SAYERS

JOHN CAMERON SWAYZE

VIVIAN VANCE

LAURA INGALLS WILDER

William Allen White (1868-1944), born in Emporia; writer, editor, publisher; known as the "Sage of Emporia"; developed the Emporia *Gazette* into one of the nation's most respected small papers; won two Pulitzer Prizes, for his editorials (1923) and his autobiography (1947); also wrote novels, short stories, and biographies of Woodrow Wilson and Calvin Coolidge

Charles Evans Whittaker (1901-1973), born in Doniphan County; jurist; U.S. Supreme Court justice (1957-62)

Laura Ingalls Wilder (1867-1957), writer; wrote a series of nine novels, known as the "Little House" books, that were based on her life growing up in the Midwest; the third book, *Little House on the Prairie*, describes her experiences as a child on the Kansas prairie

GOVERNORS

Charles Robinson	1861-1863	Harry H. Woodring	1931-1933
Thomas Carney	1863-1865	Alfred M. Landon	1933-1937
Samuel J. Crawford	1865-1868	Walter A. Huxman	1937-1939
Nehemiah Green	1868-1869	Payne Ratner	1939-1943
James M. Harvey	1869-1873	Andrew F. Schoeppel	1943-1947
Thomas A. Osborn	1873-1877	Frank Carlson	1947-1950
George T. Anthony	1877-1879	Frank L. Hagaman	1950-1951
John Pierce St. John	1879-1883	Edward F. Arn	1951-1955
George W. Glick	1883-1885	Fred Hall	1955-1957
John Alexander Martin	1885-1889	John McCuish	1957
Lyman U. Humphrey	1889-1893	George Docking	1957-1961
Lorenzo D. Lewelling	1893-1895	John Anderson, Jr.	1961-1965
Edmund Needham Morrill	1895-1897	William H. Avery	1965-1967
John W. Leedy	1897-1899	Robert Docking	1967-1975
William Eugene Stanley	1899-1903	Robert F. Bennett	1975-1979
Willis Joshua Bailey	1903-1905	John W. Carlin	1979-1987
Edward Wallis Hoch	1905-1909	Mike Hayden	1987-
Walter Roscoe Stubbs	1909-1913		
George Hartshorn Hodges	1913-1915		
Arthur Capper	1915-1919		
Henry J. Allen	1919-1923		
Jonathan M. Davis	1923-1925		
Ben S. Paulen	1925-1929		
Clyde M. Reed	1929-1931		

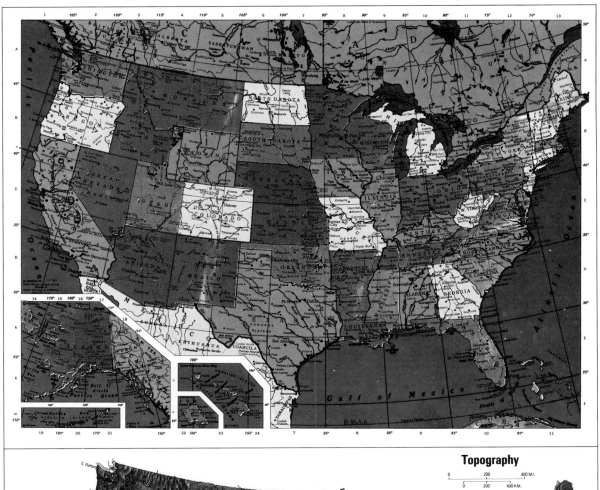

Topography

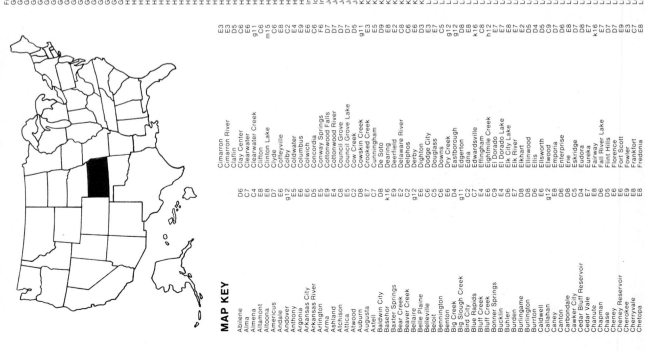

MAP KEY

From *Cosmopolitan World Atlas* © 1990 by Rand McNally, R.L. 90-S-87

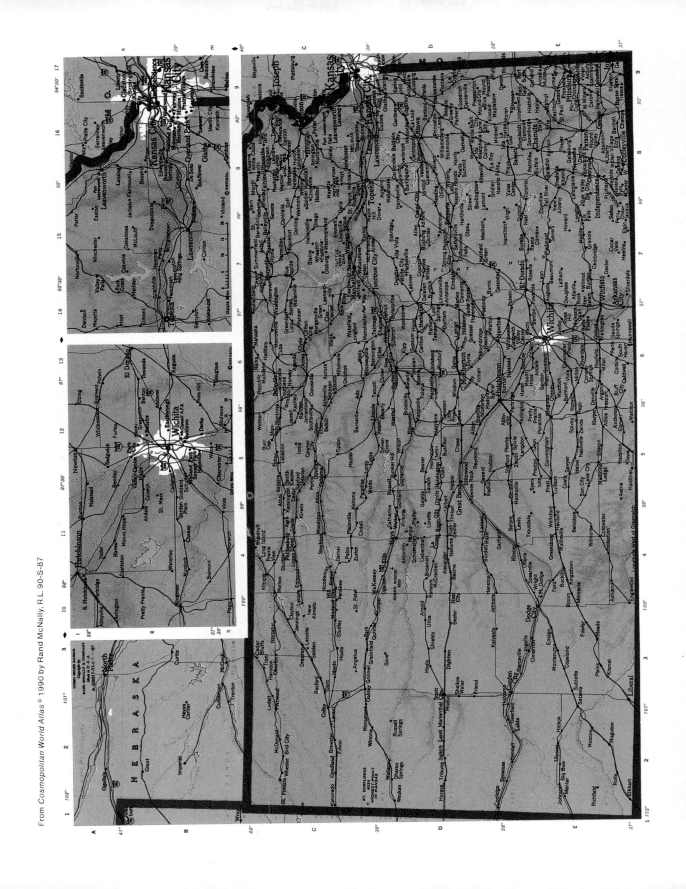

	HOGS		MANUFACTURING
	CORN		SHEEP
	BEEF		SUGAR BEETS
	POULTRY		BARLEY
	MINING		SORGHUMS
	WHEAT		DAIRY PRODUCTS
	HAY		SOYBEANS
	SALT		NATURAL GAS
	OIL		

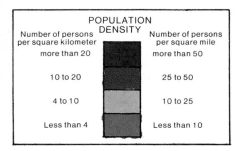

POPULATION DENSITY

Number of persons per square kilometer		Number of persons per square mile
more than 20		more than 50
10 to 20		25 to 50
4 to 10		10 to 25
Less than 4		Less than 10

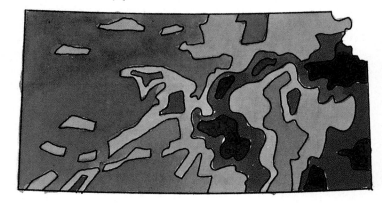

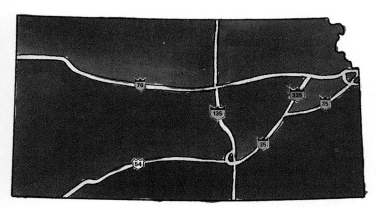

MAJOR HIGHWAYS

AVERAGE YEARLY PRECIPITATION

Centimeters		Inches
more than 91		more than 36
11 to 91		28 to 36
51 to 71		20 to 28
Less than 51		Less than 20

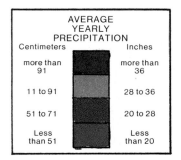

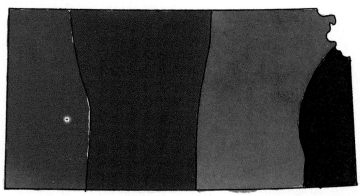

TOPOGRAPHY

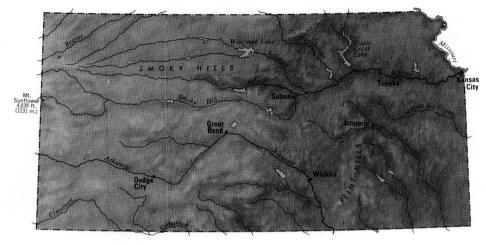

Courtesy of Hammond, Incorporated
Maplewood, New Jersey

| 5,000 m. 16,404 ft. | 2,000 m. 6,562 ft. | 1,000 m. 3,281 ft. | 500 m. 1,640 ft. | 200 m. 656 ft. | 100 m. 328 ft. | Sea Level | Below |

COUNTIES

An Independence Day parade in Lawrence

INDEX

Page numbers that appear in boldface type indicate illustrations

A Flint Hills Overland Wagon trip

Picture Identifications
Front cover: Monument Rocks
Back cover: Dodge City
Pages 2-3: Lush, rolling landscape in eastern Kansas
Page 6: Rural land in Douglas County
Pages 8-9: The rugged landscape of Clark County in southwestern Kansas
Pages 18-19: Montage of Kansas residents
Pages 24-25: *Crossing the Kansas,* a painting by Alfred Jacob Miller depicting a westward-bound American Fur Company caravan crossing the river near Lawrence in the early 1800s
Page 42: A photograph from the late 1800s of a Kansas family in front of their combination dugout-soddy
Page 60: Sunrise in Rexford
Page 72: The Kansas State Capitol in Topeka
Pages 82-83: *Sunflower Still Life,* a crop-art project by Kansas artist Stan Herd
Pages 92-93: A buffalo herd at the Maxwell Game Preserve
Page 108: Montage of state symbols, including the state flag, state tree (cottonwood), state animal (buffalo), state bird (Western meadowlark), and state flower (sunflower).

Picture Acknowledgments

Front cover, 2-3, 4, © **Dick Herpich;** 5, © **Bern Ketchum;** 6, 8-9, 11, 12, 13, © **Dick Herpich;** 14 (two photos), © **Bern Ketchum;** 15, © **Kerry Ingersoll;** 16, © **Maurice D. Norton;** 17, © **Dick Herpich;** 18 (top left, bottom right), © **Mike Yoder;** 18 (top right, bottom left), © **Joan L. Istas;** 19 (top left, top right, bottom right), © **Mike Yoder;** 19 (bottom left), © **Jim Argo;** 21, © **Mike Yoder;** 24-25, **Walters Art Gallery, Baltimore;** 28 (left), **The Kansas State Historical Society, Topeka;** 28 (right), © **Reinhard Brucker;** 32 (left), © **Bern Ketchum;** 32 (right), © **Dick Herpich;** 35, © **Janet Schleeter/R/C Photo Agency;** 36, **North Wind Picture Archives;** 38 (two photos), **The Kansas State Historical Society, Topeka;** 41, © **Wally List;** 42, 44, **The Kansas State Historical Society, Topeka;** 47, **DeGolyer Library, Southern Methodist University, Dallas;** 48, **The Kansas State Historical Society, Topeka;** 51, © **Jeff Greenberg;** 52, **The Kansas State Historical Society, Topeka;** 53, © **Cameramann International, Ltd.;** 54, 55 (two photos), **The Bettmann Archive;** 57, 58 (two photos), **The Kansas State Historical Society, Topeka;** 60, © **Dick Herpich;** 62, **The Kansas State Historical Society, Topeka;** 65, **AP/Wide World Photos;** 66, **UPI/Bettmann Newsphotos;** 67, 69, **AP/Wide World Photos;** 71, © **Jack L. Jacobs;** 72, © **Joseph Beckner/SuperStock;** 75 (left), © **Jeff Greenberg;** 75 (right), © **Dick Herpich;** 76 (left), © **Jim Argo;** 76 (right), © **Garry D. McMichael/Root Resources;** 77 (right), © **Mike Yoder;** 78, © **Cameramann International, Ltd.;** 81 (left), © **D. Dancer;** 81 (right), © **Bern Ketchum;** 82-83, © **D. Dancer;** 86, **Historical Pictures Service, Chicago;** 89 (left), illustration p. 67 from *Little House on the Prairie* by **Laura Ingalls Wilder. Illustrations by Garth Williams. Copyright 1935 Laura Ingalls Wilder, pictures copyright © 1953 Garth Williams. Reprinted by permission of HarperCollins Publishers;** 89 (right), **AP/Wide World Photos;** 90 (two photos), © **Mike Yoder;** 92-93, © **Dick Herpich;** 95, © **John Avery/Photri;** 95 (map), **Len W. Meents;** 97, © **Cameramann International, Ltd.;** 99 (left), © **Bern Ketchum;** 99 (right), © **Reinhard Brucker;** 99 (map), **Len W. Meents;** 100, © **Dick Herpich;** 102 (two photos), © **Rick Schmidt;** 102 (map), **Len W. Meents;** 104, © **D. Dancer;** 104 (map), **Len W. Meents;** 105, © **Karl Kummels/SuperStock;** 106, © **John Avery/Photri;** 107, © **D. Dancer;** 108 (tree), © **John Kohout/Root Resources;** 108 (flag), Courtesy Flag Research Center, Winchester, Massachusetts 01890; 108, (buffalo, meadowlark), © **John Avery/Photri;** 108 (sunflowers), 111, © **Dick Herpich;** 113 (left), © **Mike Yoder;** 113 (right), © **Mike Blair;** 114, © **John Avery/Photri;** 116, © **Wally Hampton/The Marilyn Gartman Agency;** 117, © **John Avery/Photri;** 119, © **Reinhard Brucker;** 120, © **Leslie A. Kelly;** 121, © **J. Blank/ H. Armstrong Roberts;** 125, **AP/Wide World Photos;** 126 (Brown), **North Wind Picture Archives;** 126 (Chrysler), **Historical Pictures Service, Chicago;** 126 (Cody, Curtis), **AP/Wide World Photos;** 127 (Dole, Earp), **Historical Pictures Service, Chicago;** 127 (Earhart, Eisenhower), **AP/Wide World Photos;** 128 (Gray), **The Kansas State Historical Society, Topeka;** 128 (Hoch), **Historical Pictures Service, Chicago;** 128 (Inge, Johnson), 129 (four photos), 130 (Menninger, Pitts, Runyon), **AP/Wide World Photos;** 130 (Nation), **Historical Pictures Service, Chicago;** 131 (Salter), **The Kansas State Historical Society, Topeka;** 131 (Sayers, Swayze, Vance), **AP/Wide World Photos;** 132, **Laura Ingalls Wilder Home Assoc.;** 136 (maps), **Len W. Meents;** 138, © **Mike Yoder;** 141, © **Bern Ketchum;** back cover, © J. Blank/**H. Armstrong Roberts**

About the Author

Zachary Kent grew up in Little Falls, New Jersey. He is a graduate of St. Lawrence University and holds a teaching certificate in English. After college, he worked for two years at a New York City literary agency before launching his writing career. He is the author of many books of American history and biography for young people.

144